Choosing Childcare

Solving your childcare problems

by

Patricia Hayes Murray

Attic Press
Dublin

© Patricia Hayes Murray 1993

First Published in Ireland in 1993 by
Attic Press
4 Upper Mount Street
Dublin 2

British Library Cataloguing in Publication Data
A catalogue record for this book is available from the British Library.

ISBN 1-855940-620

Cover Design: VanHara Design
Cover Illustration: Angela O'Hara
Origination: Verbatim Typesetting
Printing: Guernsey Press

Dedication

To the children who taught me how children think, and how to care for them, Caroline and Stephen, Ignatius, Douglas, Fergal, Dervla and Clara, Vicki, Michael and Conor, Jennifer, Gillian and Shane, Fiona, Ruadhan, Raghnaill and Vicki, Georgina, Greg, Shane and Conor. To my sister, Carmel Egan, for being such a loving aunt to my children. And to all those who lovingly care for our children.

About the Author

Patricia Hayes Murray is the mother of three children. She is chairwoman of the National Childminders' Association of Ireland. Patricia has organised numerous courses on childcare and child development over the last decade. She currently lives in Co. Wicklow.

Acknowledgements

Thank you to everybody who helped with the preparation of this book, particularly the following: Friends and colleagues who supplied ideas and source material: Anne Fawsitt, Dr Freda Gorman, Geraldine Jennings, Moira Jones, Felicity Kennedy, Elizabeth Moloney, Mary O'Brien, Marion O'Cleirigh, Carmel O'Neill, and Patricia Wojnar.

Thanks to Cian O'Tighearnaigh for permission to include the Children's Rights Charter.

Thanks to working parents who discussed their day care arrangements with me; day nurseries and childminders who welcomed me and allowed me to observe part of the day's activities; to national bodies and voluntary organisations who supplied information, annual reports and advice; to the CARI Foundation, The ISPCC and The National Rehabilitation Board for supplying publications.

To my dear husband, John, and daughter, Clara, for achieving a relative degree of self-sufficiency during the writing of this book.

Thank you also to my son, Fergal, for his help with typing and apologies to him for the inconvenience caused when using his word processor.

Thank you also to my daughter, Dervla, for her loving support and practical help with research.

Finally, I would like to thank Gráinne Healy and her colleagues in Attic Press for their helpful suggestions and courteous co-operation.

Contents

Preface

This book is a guide for working parents who are faced with the daunting task of finding day care for their babies and children. It can be a time of anxiety and frustration, when parents feel helpless, as they try to balance their ideal aspirations with what real choices are actually available to them. As I find myself spending many hours each week discussing the possible options, and the advantages and disadvantages of each type of day care with anxious parents, I realise that the time has come for setting out the information in a book.

When I got married in 1968 I retired from a busy job as Personal Assistant to the Managing Director of a big multinational company, to take care of my husband and my home. Within weeks of taking on this new role, I suffered insomnia and lay awake pondering on such household phenomena as whether taps turn on clockwise or anti-clockwise! I suppose I was longing to have a family, which did not happen for three years. My friends and neighbours had babies and toddlers. Watching them grow and develop, while hoping for one of my own, must have started my fascination.

I looked after friends' babies and children for weekends and holidays. A dear friend gave me a present of a puppy, but still I didn't sleep. All that changed when I took a job typing the theses for a group of MA students, which addressed the various aspects of the effects of poverty and disadvantage on a group of inner-city children whom they had studied. This opened my eyes to children's needs.

From my own experience of childhood, with a loving mother who understood our need for messy play, dressing up, using our heads and our hands together (before the

Montessori environment was widely known in Ireland), I knew that children needed these things. Our house was a place where children were valued, and where other children loved to come, and were welcomed.

As an adult myself, I knew that a child should have the love and respect which brings necessary self-esteem to all human beings. I could see that a child's hunger for knowledge through exploring the environment was more important than tidiness or a strict housekeeping schedule. I noticed that children were happy and easily managed, without tears or rows when I let them set the pace and duration of any activity. My job was to provide a loving and stimulating environment, where limits were kept to a minimum and only invoked in the event of wanton destruction or danger.

Typing psychology theses got me reading about child development and how children's minds work, and within a year I had two babies of my own. The insomnia vanished!

I continued providing holiday care and we always seemed to have an extra child or two in residence. I became involved in providing full day care for children of working parents and the awesomeness of the responsibility gradually dawned on me. I realised that a childminder has several functions, as well as care for her own family and home, and care for the minded children. It involved a counselling role for the young parents, sometimes liaison with social workers and teachers, and becoming involved, through the children, with visits from grannies and relatives who needed reassurance that the children were being looked after. Doing the job properly required a great variety of skills and knowledge.

Talking to other childminders we decided we should form an association and get ourselves trained. We needed a better knowledge of child development and psychology, healthcare, nutrition and even assertiveness and negotiating skills. We formed PEACH, later to become the National Childminding Association of Ireland, now a member of the International Family Day Care Organisation. With the help of the Northern Ireland and UK National Childminding Associations, we set up a course specifically designed for those involved in providing full day care.

This course helped us to a realisation of our own worth,

and encouraged us to have a professional approach to the valuable role we played in society.

I took a Diploma in Early Childhood Education, and through running the NCMAI courses and various seminars in liaison with the Department of Health, I have become a consultant in the matter of day care.

There have been great changes in the last two decades. Parents need to work and children need quality care. This book takes into account parents' feelings, and the qualities they should look for in a care-giver, as well as setting out the various options open to them. It gives practical advice about where to find the facility or person to provide the care, and solid information about interviewing and making an informed evaluation.

Finding the right person and place for your child is not always easy, but this book will help you to be clear about what you want and help you to go about getting it.

My hope is that all children will be loved, valued and respected, wherever they spend their day.

Patricia Hayes Murray
March, 1993

Dear parents

Because every family is different, the childcare arrangements which suit one family will not meet the requirements of another. Job-sharing, flexi-time and part-time work, as well as a full-time working week are possible, with the growing choice of childcare provision available.

Family needs change over time. As children grow, their needs advance from infant and toddler care, through the pre-school playgroup stage and on to after-school care. In Ireland there is very little official response to the fact that mothers want to, or need to work. But where there is a market for a service, then the opportunity arises for serving that market. Day nurseries have opened. Home-based family day care, either in the children's home or in the care provider's home is extensively used, and many courses for childcare workers are available in colleges and night classes. This offers parents a choice to match a working schedule and to fit financial resources.

If you have three or four children and a new baby, then for peace of mind as well as economic reasons you will probably need somebody to come into your home.

If you are about to have your first baby, you have many options, and *now* is the time to begin examining them. Plan ahead before the baby arrives. Talk to other parents and colleagues. Find out why they use a particular form of childcare in preference to another. There are advantages and disadvantages to be considered in all options. It takes time to make a choice and then find the person or place to suit you and your baby.

Ideally you should have made the decision about childcare before the baby arrives. You should be able to return to work (having taken as much maternity leave as possible) knowing that your baby has settled in with the care-giver, and that you trust her absolutely, whether she is in your home, or the baby is with her.

When describing childcare, the word 'interacting' appears frequently. It means being a good listener and a good talker. It involves an awareness of the child's level of language and understanding, and pitching conversation in speed of delivery and vocabulary at the child's level. It means sensitivity to a child's need for adult help sometimes, but allowing the child to experiment and solve problems at other times, without rushing in and taking over. A good care-giver knows the difference between good and bad distracting. Good distracting spots potential danger, trouble or rows and creates a successful diversion. Bad distracting is where the adult does not recognise the child's need to express feelings of anger, frustration or sadness, and a need to take time to overcome them without distraction. Bad distraction is also evident, where the adult takes too much initiative in the play-work and the child becomes the passive observer.

Interaction is knowing the subtle distinction between encouragement to complete a task, versus pressure to do so, and how and when to give appropriate praise. Interaction is sharing feelings with the children, and empathising with theirs.

The care-giver is described throughout the following chapters as female for two reasons. Firstly, female care-givers seem to be the choice of almost 100 per cent of parents because statistically children are safer with females than with males. Children have been sexually abused by females but this occurs in less than ten per cent of incidences. Secondly, it is irritating to read he/she repeatedly and we have used the generic she when talking about the baby/child.

Strong emphasis is placed, throughout this book, on obtaining and following up references and speaking to other parents who use the care-giving option you are considering. Private home-based care is completely unregulated by statute and unsupervised in Ireland. Day nurseries are subject to a minimum of inspection for suitability of persons or premises. You, as parents, must be judge and jury.

Care-givers' faults tend to be ones of omission, such as inadequate interaction, cuddling and talking to babies and children. A woman who does a lot of shouting or who threatens or slaps children has not got the necessary qualities to care for children. She will not find much satisfaction in the job, and will soon be out of patience or out of business.

As parents, you must take all possible steps to be reassured that the care-giver you have chosen raises no doubts in your mind. This is particularly important if the chosen option is home-based (either in the care-giver's home, or in the child's home) where the care-giver is unsupervised. Call unexpectedly and encourage other family members to do the same. A care-giver who comes to your home presents no difficulty as she can be checked-up upon regularly. A good childminder understands and respects your need for reassurance and information on how your child spends the day. She will be happy to see granny or aunty or you dropping in occasionally.

If you decide to have somebody caring for the baby in your home, get the arrangement started at least a week before you go back to work. If using a childminder or day nursery, leave the baby there for a few hours, to ease her into the new environment. Stay until the baby is settled on the first visit. This gives you an opportunity to get to know the care-giver a bit better than at the interview, and enables you to make the final decision that you can go to work with an easy mind.

Actually handing your baby to somebody else, no matter how satisfied you are with her, is a traumatic moment. All sorts of emotions are aroused and doubts appear. Remember, feelings cannot be helped and most parents experience the actual pang of separation. Most feel guilt as well, because society presumes that parenthood automatically, magically confers excellent parenting skills and job satisfaction, which is often far from the truth!

The unique bond between mother and the baby was given a sacred exclusiveness in the past. It made some mothers feel guilty about leaving the baby at all, or about choosing not to breast-feed. Studies of children who were separated from their mothers showed that separation affected children's later development and behaviour; but what really needed to be studied was the quality of alternative care which the children received rather than the actual separation from the mother.

Only in this century have children's needs been investigated at all. Babies need to bond with loving adults. It is essential for their growth and development. Because it is so vital, only the most extreme neglect and isolation will prevent a baby forming a special attachment to her mother, father and later to siblings or to a care-giver.

What is important is that the baby receives loving and continuous care from an individual care-giver, with whom a warm, interactive relationship develops, and in which both the baby and care-giver smile and respond to the stimulation provided by each other. Both must find joy and satisfaction in the growth of that relationship. This is what any parent requires of a care-giver.

Day nurseries are now aware of the importance of continuity of care. Some of the more enlightened are organised so that one care-giver is allocated to a specific group of babies. Three babies to any care-giver is the recommended maximum. This care-giver should move up through the stages of the nursery with her special charges, and retain that position as their 'special' person throughout their period in the nursery.

Instead of feeling guilty or jealous or threatened by the baby having a special attachment with a care-giver, parents should welcome it, as a necessary, healthy sign of development. It does not replace the unique bond that exists between a parent and child, or between siblings. Babies have always been able to extend their affection and attachment to grandparents, brothers and sisters and other relatives and friends in the extended family setting.

Motherhood for many women is associated with pain, anxiety and loss of sleep, coupled with great joy. Loss of freedom replaces the ability to move about freely, without thinking of anybody else. Even to go and buy a bar of chocolate or have a cup of coffee with a friend becomes an expedition when you have a baby. The degree of enjoyment of mothering a new baby is individual, and varies. It can be affected by the mother's own experience of being mothered when she was a child, her experience of pregnancy, the delivery, the father's response and support, her financial resources and the support of family and friends.

Some women who need to work would prefer to stay with their babies and pre-school children, while others could not imagine themselves in the role of mothering home-maker seven days a week. If you as a parent really feel the need to be at home with the baby, perhaps you could consider some alternatives or combinations of work and child-care arrangements. Could you work from home? Have you examined the possibility of job-sharing or part-time work?

You could consider caring for some other children alongside your own at home. Do some financial calculations and examine the viability. Take your net income. Deduct the cost of the childcare option you are considering. Then deduct the cost of travel to and from work, lunches, business clothes, dry-cleaning, collections for staff present-ations, the extra cost of convenience foods and take-aways. Deduct any other costs involved in your work. You may be as well-off financially by childminding even one or two extra children, or providing after-school care for older children. Your baby would benefit from the stimulation of having an older child or children around for part of the day.

If you must work outside the home, willingly or not, then you must accept the fact that feelings of guilt or sadness at separating from the baby are quite common. Feelings and emotional responses are beyond our control, and may not have been anticipated until the time to return to work actually arrives. The most practical way to deal with such feelings is to meet them head-on. If you try to bury or ignore them, they could tend to inhibit you from looking objectively, even critically, at your childcare arrangement, which should always have your alert attention. Or they may surface in the form of inappropriate anger with the care-giver, which would only make communication difficult, and would not be in the baby's interests. Do something positive. Go to the library and get a selection of books about babies, child development and day care provision. Set yourself the task of writing out ideas on childcare and child psychology which appeal to you, and which you understand as being necessary for promoting traits which you value, and which you would like to see nurtured in your child. Read about day nurseries and playgroups, so that you have clear ideas about what qualities you are looking for in these places. This exercise will give you the confidence to talk to your prospective care-giver and ask the important questions. For example, if you are considering a day nursery, what is the staff-to-child ratio? Will the baby have care continuously from one person? Can you meet her and talk to her specifically, as you would to a nanny or a childminder at an interview? Can granny or other relatives drop in occasionally? Has the day nursery got a structured play group or Montessori school?

This exercise will help you to reassure yourself that the care-giver empathises with you, and communication between you is easy. If you feel uncomfortable about anything in this person, or don't like the atmosphere in the day nursery, (this applies to a prospective childminder, and her home also), then follow your instincts and look elsewhere until you find the right person and place.

If twinges of guilt recur, make a resolution to drop a social outing and stay at home that evening, or decide there and then to give up ironing everything (except blouses and shirts, if you wish) and use the time to play with the baby or read stories. Try and avoid assuaging your feelings by over-indulging the baby or children with toys and treats. Time spent interacting, particularly with appropriate books or activities, is far more rewarding than a roomful of toys.

Because the baby's needs are best met by continuous care from one care-giver, many parents choose granny, a nanny or a childminder for the first year or so, then move a toddler to where they can interact with other children.

Somewhere between two-and-a-half and three, a pre-school playgroup is ideal, and may be available within the day nursery setting.

Current thinking suggests that children should be cared for in their own neighbourhoods, where they will get the opportunity to meet local children, and become known to people in the area. Friendships made at playgroup can follow on through school. These factors should help the individual child to have a feeling of self-worth and identify with the neighbourhood in a positive way.

From your point of view, as a parent, local day care will enable you to meet other parents who get to know your child through their children. When the time for after-school care comes, this contact will be very valuable in providing a pool of friends and schoolmates through whom you could find an appropriate after-school care arrangement.

But as a parent, the decision is yours. You have the choice of various day care options and will select the one which suits you best. Enjoy sharing the care of your baby or children and let them know how much you love them and how precious the time you share with them is.

Remember, whether you are a parent at home or out at work, bringing up children is a demanding job which offers fun and joy, but which brings some worries and doubts, not to mention the odd crisis!

The most wonderful thing about children, perhaps, is the fact that they do grow up! Worries about day care will become memories, and will, no doubt, be replaced by other worries. But in the meantime, I hope this book will be of help.

1

Profile of a good childcare provider

The first, perhaps obvious, characteristic of a good childcare provider is that she should actually like children! While very few adults are prepared to say honestly that they actively dislike children, many associate them with noise, dirt, tears and trouble!

As a survival mechanism, children are designed to be appealing, with large eyes, rosy cheeks and winsome, innocent smiles. At an emotional level, we respond warmly. But providing full time day care, like being a parent, requires more than an emotional response. Certain personality traits, allied to an even temperament, are prerequisites.

Children, from tiny babies to troubled adolescents, need affection, warmth, sympathy, approval, constancy and stability. The care-giver should have warmth of nature, self-confidence of character and a suitable temperament to meet the child's needs.

These qualities are not measurable on a scale like IQ or blood pressure. They can be observed in the manner in which the care-giver relates and responds to those around her. Eye contact, attentive listening and smiling are indicators. Body language such as firmly folded arms or fidgeting are a bad sign.

Sensitivity

To give appropriate approval and be sympathetic requires that the care-giver is sensitive. Babies and children are intuitive and readily interpret an expression, gesture or tone of voice. Generous amounts of approval, praise and encouragement, spontaneously given, will forestall a child from resorting to other tactics to attract attention. When a child uses unacceptable behaviour for the purpose of gaining attention, her need for attention must be met, as well as showing disapproval of the behaviour. These are the ongoing interactions between child and care-giver which shape the child's perception of herself and her relationship to the environment.

Constancy and stability in your child's environment can ultimately be traced to those qualities in the character of the people around her. The good care-giver will be happy with herself in her role. She will perceive her work as valuable, in the context of her own personal development, in the contribution it makes to her family income and in the wider context, as having an important function in society. She will be interested in learning more about children, through courses or reading. She will see childcare as a profession quite distinct from her role as housekeeper. This does not imply that caring for a child means carrying a baby around on her hip all the time, or kneeling all day doing jigsaws and modelling play-dough. On the contrary, children learn by observation. Watching and attempting to do the variety of household tasks in a house or day nursery interests children greatly. They copy adult activity and develop dexterity and a perception of cause and effect and an understanding of how things work. A child playing with a basin of water and a few pouring utensils of varying sizes is studying elementary physics!

Availability

Good childcare means being available to the children all the time. The child's needs must take precedence over household chores. This can mean interrupting the potato-peeling to tie a shoe lace, or get out the potty. It means listening to the children and talking to them, rather than allowing radio or television to prohibit conversation all day.

Children have a limited period in which to acquire language and this period is from birth to five years. The facility then wanes gradually and disappears during puberty. They cannot acquire language from a radio or television or from silence. After puberty, language must be learned, as we would learn a foreign language. Children acquire language in all its complexity from conversation; from a two-way interaction.

Granted, there is wide variety in the age at which language competence is reached, and boys are reputed to be slower to talk than girls. By about one year old, the baby should have some words: 'Mama; Dada; car; dog; bottle,' for example. By two, she should be putting strings together, like 'bottle all gone; me want Teddy.' Continuous progress with language is an important indicator for parents of good quality care.

Patience

Along with sensitivity, patience in a care-giver is a vital attribute. A baby takes as long as she likes to drink a bottle. Young children have no sense of time or urgency. While they are learning to do things for themselves, like feeding or washing their hands, or walking carefully up and down stairs, or getting dressed, the good care-giver will have the patience to let them make a mess, or struggle until they ask for help. She will not rush in and take over. Nor will she tidy everything up, simply because it is lunch time. The mess may represent an entire morning's work to a three-year-old, with plans for extending its scope later on. If a child is frequently fussed and hurried and frustrated, she naturally becomes resentful. She may not be able to verbalise her anger through lack of language or fear of the consequences, but she may protest by throwing a tantrum about something else — something as uncontroversial as putting on her coat or hat later on. The protest might take a more worrying form, such as refusing to eat, or reverting to babyish behaviour.

The good care-giver will always try to look at life from the child's point of view. She will recognise that the child is a human person, and will show respect accordingly. She will not walk up to a toddler unannounced and slap a wet face-cloth across her mouth, or wipe her nose without asking the child for her permission. She will not change a toddler's nappy in the public gaze of her visitors and the other children.

Support

Feelings cannot be helped, and a child is entitled to feel cross, tired, afraid, lonely or excited. Care-givers will avoid the negative put-downs like 'don't be silly; bold; spoilt; cross'. If a child is terrified of spiders, the care-giver will respond by saying: 'Yes, they do look really frightening, but they don't hurt us, they run away from us.' This validates the child's feelings and then gives the necessary reassurance. Above all, she will never tell a child to stop crying. She will realise that children only cry when they need to. They may need comfort or they may need to express disappointment or frustration. But they need to cry until they stop.

In order to deal with feelings, children need to express them. If feelings are ridiculed or dealt with unsympathetic-ally, they may be buried. But, feelings buried are buried alive, and will definitely re-surface later, maybe years later, in unacceptable antisocial behaviour.

Security

The care-giver must be secure in herself. This enables her to apologise to a child if she has made a mistake, and to say 'please' and 'thank you'. Being secure and having a feeling of self-worth prevents authoritarian or pompous attitudes.

Of course an adult has power, authority and might in relation to a child, but they count for nothing when compared with the results of sharing feelings honestly with a child. If a care-giver finds something is funny or sad or boring, let her say so. Real security and self-esteem come from truth and respect for a child's deep feelings and from the child's observation of those traits in the role-models around her.

Touch

The good care-giver will know that it takes about eight seconds to pick up a child and tell her 'you're great and I love you.' To do this eight times a day takes just over one minute, but the rewards are infinite. Words like 'bold; bad; naughty' disappear. The child gets the message that the care-giver's love is constant and enduring, irrespective of day-to-day transgressions and misdemeanours. Love and approval will not be withdrawn or only measured out in response to perceived 'good behaviour.' The brightest, dullest, most wilful or wildest child gets the message about feeling secure with a care-giver very quickly and it underlies the relationship between child and care-giver, and ultimately, between the child and other people.

Discipline

Discipline only has a lasting value when it becomes self-discipline. Like most other skills, children learn it through observation. The care-giver will exhibit this by being organised, anticipating needs and averting trouble. She must never express anger by smacking a child. She must not regulate behaviour by frightening or threatening the children. Children treated in this way will introduce their own defence mechanisms, and will learn to become deceitful and manipulative to keep the peace. She should not threaten sanctions which she does not intend to carry out. She should reserve shouting for emergencies, like warning of potential danger. She should not undertake to care for so many children that she is frequently overworked and irritable.

Practicality

Tolerance of difference is another necessary quality in a good care-giver. Sharing the care involves seeing the parents' attitudes as valid, not necessarily right or wrong, just different. The care-giver will realise that parents will deal with things their way at home. She will want to offer consistency to the child by following through with parents' practice in areas such as table manners, potty training or answering questions like 'Where do babies come from?' The up-tight, always-right, bossy, controlling individual will not provide good childcare.

Trust

Accepting responsibility and trust between employer and employee is a necessary component of any job. These are vital in a childcare-giver. The parents must feel secure that she will not try to mislead or deceive them in any way. If the child has a fall or gets a fright, the parents should be told. If the care-giver thinks a child is falling behind the developmental milestones for her age (see page 100), or if she is unable to discourage unacceptable behaviour such as biting other children, she must talk to the parents and a team approach towards finding a solution should be sought.

Sense of humour

Above all, anybody caring for children needs a sense of humour. Children need fun and laughter. They love jokes, puns and playing creatively with language. As among adults, difficult situations can be negotiated and embarrassment can be diffused with humour. A good care-giver will see the funny side of finding a sausage in her handbag at the bank, or a row of spiders drawn in felt-tip on the wallpaper behind the sofa. She will be able to laugh at herself when she says or does or wears something which the children find funny. A good sense of humour recognises that ridicule or teasing is not funny at all, and laughter is a two-way process.

Training

All the foregoing might appear to be the profile of a saint, and impossible to find among the world of mortal women! But there has been an increased awareness of children's needs and understanding of how their minds work during the past forty years. Childcare colleges with two year and three year full-time courses have come into existence. Many evening courses in childcare and development, child psychology and parenting skills are available.

With women's contribution to the workforce increasing in value, particularly in Europe; and with declining populations, childcare provision is increasingly perceived as a valuable career option, and recognised as requiring a high level of motivation and a variety of natural skills, as well as training.

It is not suggested that children will fail to achieve their potential if a teenage neighbour or cousin cares for them occasionally for pocket money. But parents who are looking for full day care provision must realise that they are sharing the parenting role. Children will be influenced by a full-time care-giver, and will build up a strong affectionate relationship with her. This is healthy and necessary for their day-to-day happiness. Parents may feel an uncomfortable response to this notion at first. But as the child grows and the loving bond with parents develops, they will understand that the extension of affection by the child to her care-giver, extended family and friends, is a most natural and welcome development.

If children are treated fairly, with tolerance, patience and approval, they will develop and practice these traits in their relationships with others throughout their lives, and will grow in self-confidence and security. As young adults, they will have a feeling of self-worth which will be evident in qualities like courage and integrity, and taking responsibility for their actions. They will have the tools to achieve their full potential, and will not be held back, or easily led into trouble by self-doubt or low self-esteem.

2

Options for day care

Family day care - the childminder

Although the name 'childminder' is used to describe live-in or live-out childcare providers, a childminder providing day care in the home (not a relative) is usually a mother who takes other children into her home during the day. In US and in the UK, where statistics are available and where childminders are registered, this type of family day care provision is the most frequently used by working parents. It is also valued by social services as an appropriate setting for children with special needs, and for children of parents under stress.

In Ireland, where there is no registration of childminders, we can only extrapolate that it is very popular here also. The perception among many parents is that if children cannot be in their own home all day, then another home, with one mother-figure and the atmosphere and flexibility of home life, is a good alternative. When the childminder has a flair for the job – if she is genuinely fond of babies and children and has the temperament and patience to do the job well, then it is a very good alternative.

If you can find a childminder living nearby, then the baby has the advantage of growing up in her neighbourhood. When play-school or big-school time comes, there will be friends and old playmates and neighbours among the sea of strange faces.

A childminder offers a one-to-one relationship, which is ideal for the baby in the first year of life, and which is not always possible in day nurseries where the child care is given in a nursery setting, not in a home.

Finding a childminder

- The best way to find a good childminder is by word of mouth.
- Are any of your neighbours or friends working parents who could recommend one?
- Is there a local pre-school playgroup or mother and toddler group where you could meet other young mothers and ask them?
- Talk to mothers who work in the local bank, shops, schools or industrial estates.
- Personal recommendation is the best introduction.
- You may be forced to advertise. Look for childminders advertising their services in the local papers, or on notice boards in the locality.

Once you have singled out a possible childminder the next step is to arrange to visit her, in her home. Try and do this during the day, when she has her own children, and other minded children around. The environment in which the baby develops will influence her, and parents should be able to imagine themselves as children spending each day with this person, in this house. Think back to your own childhood. Do you remember how you loved spending hours in some friends' houses, and on the other hand, felt somewhat uncomfortable or unwelcome in others? Try to put your finger on what made you feel at ease then.

Don't rush through the visit to the prospective childminder's home. If she is the right person to care for the baby, she will appreciate your need to take your time. She will value the opportunity to assess you as people with whom she will become intimately involved through sharing the care of your child. She must also have the opportunity to assess you as future employers. If she does not make you feel welcome and relaxed, you have no reason to think that your child will feel any differently. Remember, this is your first time going through this experience. She has been there before, with other first-timers, like yourselves. It is her responsibility, and also a measure of her professionalism to make the interview a pleasant as well as an informative experience for you. She can do this by being forthcoming with an offer to look over the house and see the area available to the children. She can give you some idea of how many children she has, and how many she looks after. But she should not give a one hour monologue, leaving you no time or opportunity to ask the questions which are important to you!

First impressions of childminder

Be observant. What sort of person is this childminder?

- Has she clean hair and fingernails and clothes?
- Does she smoke?
- Is she very overweight or very underweight?
- Does she, and her children look healthy?
- Can she make conversation easily?
- How does she interact with the children?
- Does she handle well the situation of needing a bit of peace to talk to you?
- Can she cope calmly? You must allow that children 'act up' when visitors appear.
- Do her own children appear secure?
- Can you imagine her reading a story with a bit of animation, or cuddling a teething baby?
- Is she a good listener?
- Does she avoid eye contact?

First impressions of the house

- Ask to look around the house. Untidiness is perfectly acceptable to children because it is a by-product of their play activity.
- Danger, dirt or chaos is a different matter.
- Are there toys, books, musical instruments?
- Is the house obviously geared for children, with guards on fires, potties and a child-step for using the toilet, and a gate at the stairs?
- Has she a quiet room for children to sleep during the day, with clean bedclothes?
- Is the garden secure, with a sand pit, swings or slides, or climbing frames?
- Is there a pot-guard on the cooker and a fire blanket or extinguisher in the kitchen?
- Do you notice any overloaded sockets or trailing flexes?

It is not suggested that you eliminate a prospective childminder on the basis of any one of these observations. They are pointers which make up a picture of her character and environment. A woman's home is her castle and her private domain. It is not subject to public scrutiny in the same way as a day-nursery is. You alone, as parents, have the responsibility of deciding on the basis of what you see and hear, if this is the right person and place for your child.

If you notice that the house is immaculate, with every ornament in place and not a mark on a wall, or fingerprints on the fridge, or a dent in a cushion, or a shadow on a plain cream or beige carpet, or at least one curtain hanging askew — Beware! This is not a house where children are happy and busy.

On the other hand, if you are at ease with this woman, and are satisfied with her home, you must ask some questions. She will expect this, and should not appear on the defensive.

Interview questions to ask childminders

- What experience has she had as a mother and childminder?
- Can you have a reference from parents of other minded children and from her family doctor?
- Is she insured for childminding?
- Has she attended any courses in child development and first aid?
- How many under-fives are there in the house, including her own children?
- Has she a phone?
- If she has a car, does her insurance policy cover minded children?
- What does she charge?
- Is she flexible about collecting time?
- What is included in her charge – meals, making up bottles, some laundry?
- Has she or her family had any serious illness?
- What charge does she make if the baby is sick, or during holidays?
- If she is a member of the National Childminding Association using their contract form? (See p133).
- Will she bring the baby to the clinic for developmental checks and vaccinations?
- Will she bring and fetch older children to and from play-school or big-school?

Add your own questions to the list:

-

-

-

-

-

The childminder: check her out

Obviously it is in your child's interest that she has experience with children of her own, even if she is a first-time childminder. If this is the case, ask for a character reference as well as a family doctor's reference. One of her children's teachers or the local public health nurse, who will have had access to her house and who will have a record of her children on file would be useful. As with all references from potential childcare workers, you must follow them up. You must satisfy yourselves as far as possible that she is not misleading you in any way, or holding back any important information. In the UK and northern Ireland a police check is run on the household, in case the spouse or older children have been in trouble with the law. You are entitled to do the same at the local police station. If the woman has been childminding, follow up the references from parents of other minded children by talking to them about your prospective childminder.

Ordinary household insurance does not include minded children. Cover for minding children *is* available and she should have a certificate of cover.

If the childminder has a professional approach to the job, or, as a mother, is interested in child development or child psychology, she may have attended some relevant course. However, if you notice a shelf of books on childcare and development and the house contains some obviously well cared for children, with plenty of toys, play materials, books, dressing-up clothes and baby equipment — don't press too hard for qualifications. Practical experience and the right temperament are the most important requisites for undertaking child care. However, you could ask what she would do if a baby swallowed a penny, or started to choke, or developed a high temperature just to check out her responses to such questions.

Ask the childminder what she includes in her job, such as dinner, making up bottles, keeping spare clothes laundered, or bringing the child to the clinic or playschool. Ask her to describe a typical day in her house. As well as helping you decide whether she is the childminder for you and your child, the more you discuss beforehand the less likely you are to be surprised or annoyed later. It is not good for children to be chopped and changed from one carer to another, so minor difficulties and differences must be ironed out. Now is the time to assess how easy the minder is to talk to. If you can't get two words out of her or if you can't get her to draw a breath while you ask her a question — will she be easy to communicate with on an ongoing basis!

Ratio of minder to children

How many pre-school children should a minder care for? This depends on the ages of the children, and on the minder herself. Not more than three under-fives is the rule of thumb, and the legal requirement in the UK. But a minder with, say a two-year-old and two three-and-a-half year olds who perhaps go to playschool from 9.30 am to 12.00, would probably be able to care for a baby or another toddler. Without state regulation, you as parents must make a judgement on what seems reasonable and safe.

Mobility and contactability

What is important is that the minder must be mobile — be able to take the children to the shops, or for a walk. If she has too many small children, she will be house-bound, and one of the great advantages of family care is lost. Children learn about the world by being taken to the shops, the bank, the library, the hairdressers, the post office. Like adults, they need variety in everyday-life. A good childminder will understand this need and ensure that she provides a wealthier environment than merely a place of safe containment all day.

A phone is necessary where one person alone is childminding. It is reassuring for both parents and childminder to have ready and direct contact, and it is essential should any emergency arise.

If the childminder has a car and part of her job is to collect and deliver minded children or drive them to school or activities, check that she is adequately insured and that the car is not dangerously overloaded with children. While you are visiting take a good look at the car. Bald tyres or broken lights may suggest bad brakes. If you don't like the look of the car, say you'd prefer if your child was not driven in it.

Rates of pay

The rates of pay for a family child-minding vary from one area to another, and are linked to other socio-economic factors. In poorest circumstances a childminder may mind several children for poorly-paid parents for a few pounds per day. At the other end of the scale, a minder may take only one child in at a time and charge about £70 per week. The average minder, with a house and garden available to the children, charges between £50 and £60 per week. Extra charges for leaving children later than the agreed collection time *must* be paid for. Usually, a reduction is made for more than one child from the same family. Discuss the pay arrangements, cash or cheque, weekly or monthly — and stick to them!

The minder is entitled to payment when the child is sick or on holidays. If parents are teachers, enquire about holding the place with the childminder over the summer months.

Rules

While the childminder at home is perceived as being more flexible about collection time than a day nursery or workplace nursery, do not take this for granted. Remember, the childminder has her own family to attend to. They will not take kindly to having dinner or homework interrupted regularly by you arriving late. If you know your job involves working late regularly, discuss this with the minder at the outset and make the financial agreement accordingly. Remember your child's needs at the end of a long day in this context. Her day can be structured to a certain extent, but the childminder can only do this with a realistic collection time in mind.

If you feel shy to ask whether the minder or her family have had any serious illnesses, then check out with her family doctor when verifying the reference. Ask the doctor point blank if she is a suitable candidate for childminding – mention depression, heart condition and hypertension as being relevant.

If the minder is a member of the National Childminding Association she will give you a contract to sign. (See sample, Appendix I page 133). Take it home and read it. This gives you the opportunity to think over the interview, your impressions of the childminder and her home and children. You can note any questions you forgot to ask and raise them when bringing back the contract. She should also provide you with a form seeking information about the child, such as vaccination records, special diet requirements, pet hates or phobias, your work and home phone numbers, family doctor. (Note: copies of this information sheet are to be found in Appendix 2, page 135)

Staying informed

Close communication between the parents and the childminder is in the child's best interest. Because children invariably 'act out', show off or throw a tantrum when a parent arrives at collection time, and because the childminder has come to the end of her day's work and has other commitments to attend to – this is not the time to have a discussion about potty training, or saying grace before meals, or biting! It may embarrass or annoy an older child to witness or overhear this discussion. The best policy is to agree to the fortnightly phone call, evening time or weekend, in advance. This puts the structure in place for calm, reflective discussion of any problems that may arise with the child's behaviour, or dissatisfaction with each others' performance among the adults. An expected phone call has no inherent threatening or accusing overtones. Finding the reason for unacceptable behaviour, and ironing out difficulties or differences between the adults is the objective – and not trying to attach blame.

No care-share arrangements will be without some

difficulties. It is in the best interests of all parties that good communication is the vehicle for overcoming them. Remember, the childminder may have much more experience of children than the parents, and the parents know their child's nature in a unique way. The solution to difficulties lies in combining the two, and this is done by listening attentively to each other.

While far-sighted parents will be actively organising day care before the baby is born, if you already have a baby or child or children when visiting the prospective childminder, bring them with you. Observe how she responds to them, and they to her. A warm spontaneous enthusiasm for children, and the ability to put them at their ease is a necessary quality in a good child care-giver. Like nursing or teaching it is a job to be undertaken by those with a flair and feeling for it.

Current thinking is that ideally, the day care facility should be located in the child's neighbourhood. As well as making delivery and collection easier for the parents, this arrangement allows the child to grow up in her locality and to identify with it and the people who live there. This is an important part of personality development.

If possible, even with a young baby, try and arrange with the childminder to bring baby/child/ren along for a couple of short periods before you return to work. This is helpful for everybody. The children will begin to feel at home, and the childminder can note their individual requirements and talk to you about them. You can then make the final decision as to whether this is the right childminder for you.

Advantages of a non-family member childminder:
• The child gets continuity of care from one person
• The child grows up in a home from home
• There are other children in the environment
• The child can be taken out and about
• The childminder's home bears the wear and tear on house and furnishings
• You keep home a strictly private place

Disadvantages:
- Family day care is unregulated in Ireland
- Parents must satisfy themselves as to suitability of the person and the premises
- Can be costly
- Parents have no control over who enters childminder's home

Granny as childminder – live in

In the extended family, interdependence gave granny a role in childminding. The children, ideally, developed a strong bond with granny, and were in turn able to help care for her when she became more dependent through age or illness. If you have a resident granny who is healthy, and happy to care for baby, then maybe you need not read any further!

But just as times have changed for mothers in a society which values their contribution in the workforce, grannies are not necessarily home makers or redundant child-rearers. Granny may have a job too, or a garden which she enjoys, or community work commitments, or she may be a scratch golfer. She may let it be known early and clearly that her freedom is precious and the young working parents may look elsewhere for childcare.

But if granny can't wait to get her hands on baby because she genuinely likes babies and small children and enjoyed the mothering role with her own children, then things are looking good!

Now, you must be fair – fair to granny, fair to the baby, and fair to yourself. Sharing the care of the baby involves parents in a unique, intimate relationship with whoever shares the care. Sensibilities and sensitivities are aroused, and it can be quite difficult for a young parent to question the practices of any care-giver.

Asking granny leading questions can only bring the response: 'And what's wrong with the way I reared you lot?' Subject closed!

So how can young parents be fair to granny?

Let us imagine that she is willing to care for the baby, and she lives with you or you live with her. Ask yourself is she fit and well? Feeding and changing and cuddling a new baby is not particularly arduous, but changing a nappy for a strong, active eight-month-old, or carrying her upstairs is strenuous activity. Because it is important that the baby should not have a succession of care-givers, particularly in the first year, you must look ahead with granny.

Does she have fond memories and stories about you as babies and young children? If she has other older grandchildren – do they like her? Is she tolerant, patient and not easily fussed? Has she a good sense of humour and is she able to see another person's point of view?

If, on the other hand, she is a controlling personality, capable and efficient, perhaps, but always right, maybe life could be difficult for everybody.

How did you/your partner fare? Have you reached a reasonable level of independence and normality in adolescence and young adulthood?

Talk to granny beforehand about what's important to you. Remember, babies cannot have too much love and cuddles – that is what they thrive on. It does not spoil them. The more cuddles they get as infants, the less inappropriate, attention-seeking behaviour they will exhibit later on. Granny is most likely to offer this loving spontaneously.

If she has hard and fast principles of child-rearing, make sure that they are roughly in line with your own. A vast amount of development takes place in the first year of the baby's life. A small, helpless bundle, who knows only how to suck, becomes a walking, still small, but independent-minded human being. Such rapid change requires flexibility to meet the baby's changing needs.

Is granny the kind of person you can communicate with easily? Will the baby be able to let her know that she is exhausted from smiling and wants a snooze, or that she's not hungry, wet, bold or spoilt, but just wants company – a chat and a cuddle?

You can't interview granny. She's just granny, and she is there and willing. But you **do** have responsibilities as a parent.

Questions about granny

• Are her eyesight and hearing still good?
• How would she cope with an emergency?
• Is she on any medication which might make her drowsy or forgetful, such as sleeping pills, or anti-depressants?
• Does she leave a handbag full of pills lying around?
• Does she drink on her own?
• Does she smoke heavily?
• Has she a jealous dog or cat?
• Would she need some help with the extra washing and housework which a baby produces?
• Has she high blood pressure or a heart condition?
• Is grandad around, well and active, or does he need caring for?
• Would the demands of a baby and grandad be too much for granny to cope with?

If anything about granny raises doubts about the baby's safety and welfare, or about granny's own health and sanity, follow your instincts. Be kind, be firm, be assertive, but *don't* go to work each day with a gnawing uneasiness. Frequent telephone calls to check on things at home may make the situation worse, and they will definitely irritate your colleagues or business partners. This holds true for whatever childcare arrangements you make.

Deciding that you don't want to leave the baby with granny and making other plans may have difficult repercussions in the family context, but be careful not to simply drift into granny as care-giver, or be emotionally blackmailed into it, because it is the one care-share situation which you will not drift out of easily!

Granny's needs

No matter how willing and delighted to do the job granny

is, do not take her for granted. It is a job and she must be paid. Her circumstances and yours will be individual and you may wish to barter gardening, house-decorating, or shopping for childcare. But stick to the arrangements you make. Sporadic treats are not entitlements.

- Granny *is* entitled to payment for her work, just like anybody else.
- Be sensitive to her needs, as well as the baby's.
- Listen attentively to her.
- Is she trying to tell you she finds the job lonely, or too tiring?
- Is baby-care more difficult than she had imagined or remembered? Is she slightly resentful of your freedom and lifestyle?

Perhaps everybody would be happier if granny didn't undertake full day care of the baby, but filled the necessary and valuable support role. She could be on stand-by, in case the baby or usual care-giver is sick. She might share the job with some other type of day care such as a student or au pair. She may be a night-owl, and enjoy babysitting, rather than becoming involved in the household chores.

Like any other childcare arrangements, live-in granny has its pluses and minuses.

Advantages of live-in granny as a childminder:
- You know her
- She has both your and the baby's best interests at heart
- She'll give the love that the baby needs in a unique way
- She'll probably be flexible about working late
- No driving the baby morning and evening
- The baby stays in her own home

Disadvantages:
- Granny may be set in her ways
- She may resume mothering the parents
- She may interfere and undermine the parents
- She may not be really able for the job

Granny as childminder – non-live in (baby stays at home)

Suppose granny does not live with you, and has offered to come to your home each day. The imaginary interview with granny still holds good – but what other factors come into play? (questions, see Chapter One).

You are young adults, with your own home and privacy, you are relatively free from parental advice or interference. Would you or your partner be quite happy to let granny have the run of the house? You won't have time to hide that incriminating bank statement before she arrives in the morning. She might find out that your housekeeping standards leave a lot to be desired. She might find fur on the back of the fridge and lock the dog out all day. She might see the brochures and know you've made holiday plans before you have even decided whether you can afford to go or not. She might become intimately friendly with the neighbour and have her calling in regularly. She may be motivated by the desire to save the baby from its heathen, materialistic, fun-loving, irresponsible parents, and feed subversion to the baby, along with the baby rice and mashed bananas.

The above nightmare scenario is really to alert you to the fact that granny will be unable to resist mothering you – the parents – along with the baby.

Will granny require to be collected and left home at the start and end of a busy day? Or will someone else call each evening to collect her, and stay for two hours!

If granny never got up to go out to work five days a week, is it a realistic proposition to expect her to start such a career at a time when people normally think of retiring?

But flip the coin and think of the good side of mothering to be found in granny.

> • She may be a home maker as well as a nanny.
> • She'll light the fire and prepare a meal.
> • She may bake and sew.
> • She'll welcome you and make your tea after a murderous day.
> • She loves you as well as the baby, and will want to express that love her way. Be wise and gentle, appreciate her and praise her efforts. If she does not do things exactly the way you would — well, there are more ways than one. If she is happy, and the baby is happy, then don't you be unhappy.

Decide what is important and necessary for granny to do and talk to her beforehand. If she has the energy and enjoys doing lots more, notice it and be grateful, but if she is undertaking a marathon each day, then tell her gently and frequently that she and the baby are what really matter.

Advantages of granny coming to your home as childminder:

• You know her extremely well
• She'll probably be flexible about working late
• No driving the baby morning and evening
• Baby stays at home

Disadvantages:

• Collecting granny and bringing her home
• Granny may be set in her ways
• She may resume mothering the parents
• She may interfere and undermine the parents
• She will be another presence in your home each evening/ morning

Granny as non-live-in childminder: In granny's home

Is sending the baby to granny to be minded a realistic option? The baby is now going out each morning to fit into granny's world and lifestyle. Did she offer to care for the baby in a great gush of emotion when she held her at the bedside and remembered you all those years ago, when she was a young ecstatic mum herself? Did she forget about her usual day-to-day undertakings and social life? Will she be too tired to go out in the evenings or to play golf or bowls at the weekend? If this is to be an option, think and talk it through well in advance before the baby appears, and definitely before the baby first smiles at granny.

Is bringing the baby to granny practical in terms of distance? Getting the baby up and fed, (and you can't hurry a baby) getting yourself ready for work and facing a journey with one eye on the baby and one on the clock is the stuff accidents and heart attacks are made of. If you are seriously considering this option do a few dry runs at the appropriate hour some mornings before the baby arrives and see what the reality is. Try a wet morning when traffic is at its worst.

If granny is your first choice, then get organised. Keep a set of the baby's requisites in granny's. You don't use any more by keeping a dual supply on the go. Get a second carrycot, high chair, buggy and playpen (usually easy to borrow) and don't risk breaking your back hauling these things in and out of the car each day.

Let granny make up all the bottles, and bring her back the empties. Don't be selfish! When the baby needs sleep, she must not be kept awake by granny so the baby can show you a new trick.

Look at books on childcare and development and when you find one that makes common sense to you — buy two copies, one for granny and one for you, and ask granny's opinion about the practices suggested. This is a gentle way of letting granny know about up-to-date safe childcare, and a tactful way of getting your ideas on potty-training, diet, or discipline across. You don't have to agree with everything in the book, but it is important that you and granny are of one mind on these types of issues.

Is granny's home geared for a child? Is she overly houseproud? Has she replaced the furnishings and carpets (which you lot demolished) with powder blue and light beige ones? Has she a wonderful and treasured collection of china and glass ornaments? The baby should not be subjected to five years of 'Wash your hands, wipe your feet, don't touch, put it down, put it back, leave it alone!'

Does granny live in a very settled neighbourhood, where there are few children around? This could make life lonely for a developing toddler.

Remember that granny's electricity and heating bills will increase and she may have other out-of-pocket expenses. These must be taken into consideration when coming to the financial arrangements.

If the baby goes to granny's home and both granny and the baby are getting along fine, another doubt may creep into your head. Granny may have been willing from the beginning of the arrangement to keep the baby overnight, if the parents were working late or wanted a night out. Granny might get the idea into her head that the baby is somehow happier or less disturbed by staying frequently overnight with her. This may just happen gradually, imperceptably. Before a tug-of-love arises, parents should be aware of the signs.

Granny may start to compare her care-giving with that of the parents, with a veiled or even open suggestion that her care is more favourable for the baby.

This is the time to be calm, firm and assertive. Bring the baby home, and don't discuss the issue within her hearing. Remember you do not have to give a dozen reasons to anybody as to why you want your child at home. Simply say you miss them too much when an overnight is spent in granny's. It is also a time to let granny know how you value the unique loving care which she gives the baby. Try not to over-react by stopping overnighting completely. That is not necessary and will not bring granny around to your point of view. It is simply a matter of re-establishing **you** as parent.

Advantages of baby going to granny for childminding:
• You know her extremely well
• She'll probably be flexible about working late

- No phone/heat/light bills running up in your house during the day
- You keep your home a private place

Disadvantages:
- Delivering and collecting the baby
- The baby will not be living in her own locality
- Settled neighbourhood may be short of playmates
- Granny may begin to think that the baby should live with her.

Sister\in-law as childminder

Like granny, when choosing your sister/partner's sister as a childminder, you know the person well. If she has children, you probably can see how she relates to them and assess their growth and general development.

But remember, all the factors discussed in relation to non-family childminders will come into play. It may be more difficult to discuss problems or contentious areas with your sister than with a stranger.

Remember that you will be entering a business arrangement with your sister. Both parties must recognise this and respect it, or the sisterly affection may become strained!

Read the section here on the childminder (Chapter One), and apply it to your sister. Obviously, you will not need a reference or do a police check, but she should love children and have the appropriate qualities required to undertake childminding.

Questions to be considered:

- Is she insured?
- How many under-fives are in her care?
- Can she take them out?
- Is her house geared for children and the garden secure?

Don't just jump into the arrangement without careful consideration; remember the mental interview (Chapter One).

As with granny, or a neighbour or friend as childminder — if things go wrong and you decide to make other day care arrangements, your sister will be your sister and you will not easily be able to avoid her!

Childcare arrangements should not be changed without a serious reason. If you are dissatisfied with your sister's care for your child, you must be truthful and at the same time avoid being hurtful. Don't get into passing judgement or assigning blame. Be honest in saying how sorry you are that the arrangement did not work for your child.

Be rigid in refusing to discuss the matter with any other family members, even if your sister tries to involve them, and tell her that you are sticking to that policy. Do not discuss the situation, or make any derogatory remarks about your sister within earshot of your child.

As with using a neighbour or friend as a childminder, ending the arrangement will have implications for the relationship. Only persistent goodwill on your part, and reassurance that you value the sisterly affection between you, will heal the perceived insult in time.

Don't try to avoid your sister. Keep the lines of communication open, showing that you are willing to put the past behind you. Make a conscious effort to speak to the child about your sister's positive qualities and direct the child's attention to the advantages of the new day care arrangement.

Advantages of sister as childminder:
- You know your sister well
- An affectionate family bond exists
- Child has the opportunity to form close family ties with cousins
- She will probably keep the child later than arranged without difficulty

Disadvantages:
- Changes the sisterly relationship to a business one
- She can begin to get bossy

- She can try to 'take over' the mothering of your child
- She may think she has a right to criticise your life/lifestyle
- Discussing money/contractual arrangement may be difficult

Neighbour as childminder

Having a neighbour as a childminder may seem ideal, for the child and parents. Even a child who is not well can be taken next door (if the neighbour is agreeable). The difficulty lies in the fact that parents need to have the same information about a neighbour as set out in relation to the childminder (Chapter One). If your neighbour offers to care for your child, can you ask her whether she has any training in childcare and development? Can you ask to see her car insurance or suggest that she show you references?

Make sure you know the neighbour well. You will have had the advantage of observing her children at close quarters over a period of time. What do you think of them? If they are destructive little horrors and you have heard her shouting at them continually through the wall, then perhaps look elsewhere. If she is already childminding, you can make contact with the parents of children already in her care.

You will have seen more of her home environment and obviously know her better than somebody contacted through an advertisement or by word of mouth. But be very sure that you are happy with her, because, as with granny and sister, if things do not work out and you wish to make other arrangements, the neighbourly quality of the relationship may suffer.

Family day care arrangements between friends tend to be hazardous to either the friendship or, to the child care arrangement. Negotiating a prior relationship, such as one between yourself and a neighbour or friend into one involving exchange of money for services can be difficult. The arrangement may be cancelled to save the friendship, or the friendship may be lost if the new business arrangement does not work out. A breakdown in arrangements will be difficult enough for adults to cope with, but it will have a confusing effect on the child.

Inadequacies in a childminder may come to a parent's attention by neighbours of that childminder. The motivation for such reporting should always be questioned. It may be malicious, or arise from neighbourly dissatisfaction with noise, or parents thoughtlessly parking while calling to the childminder. But a neighbour who has observed neglect or danger to minded children might be reluctant to report to the parents. In any childcare situation, such reports should always be followed up by the parents, after cautious enquiry and investigation.

When a child can get about under her own steam and is able to go to the childminder's house unaided, outside the hours of the arrangement, parents must address this development.

The childminder may say that she understands perfectly the child's perception that her home is viewed by the child as a second home, and that she does not object. But parents must be very sensitive to the fact that the childminder's own children have needs. They should be guaranteed time as a family without having to share their mother, their home and their possessions with other children. Her partner may not be charmed by your child feeling free to come in any time. The childminder can find herself caught in a complex triangle, and be reluctant to set limits in case she upsets her relationship with your child, or causes offence which could upset the business arrangement.

The childminder is a professional and cannot switch off from that commitment at weekends. She is aware that she cannot leave your child unattended by her in her house, in a situation where it would be reasonable to leave her own children, such as with an older child in charge.

Parents should take the lead, bring the child home and explain in simple terms that firstly, she is precious to them and they miss her during the working time, and want to be with her when free. Secondly, the childminder needs to have her family time with her children, and it is only fair to allow that.

Parents should ask the childminder to explain the situation to the child in similar terms. Like all difficulties which arise, a combined, consistent, clear message from both parents and care-giver prevents the child from becoming confused by conflicting signals, and leaves little room for any 'divide and conquer' tactics on the child's part.

Where the childminder has children of a similar age to yours, a certain amount of neighbourly coming and going to each other's houses is normal and only becomes a problem when the traffic is one-way. Children don't apply the maxim that good fences make good neighbours, so the adults must use common sense in setting limits. Taking the initiative and responsibility rests on the parents of the minded child.

If you have sound reasons for discontinuing the childcare arrangement with a neighbour, the following factors must be borne in mind.

- Make sure you have the alternative arrangement in place.
- Check the contract for commitments to give notice or payment in lieu on termination of the arrangement.
- In the interest of neighbourly relations continuing, focus on the child's needs, rather than the childminder's inadequacies, when telling her you have made alternative arrangements. These will vary in each particular situation and could be a child's need for more interaction with other children of the same age or a child's need for individual care, if the childminder cares for a few children.
- Be warned that the neighbourly relationship will suffer. The duration and severity of the cooling-off period will depend on the reason for ending the arrangement. Whatever the circumstances, say plainly that you are sorry that things did not work out, but your responsibility for your child's care takes precedence over everything and you hope that you can continue to be good neighbours.

Reassure the childminder that the relationship between you was a private matter, and you will not discuss it with other neighbours or in front of the child.

You must also be aware of the effects of the move on your child. If the child is old enough to understand, have your explanation rehearsed and don't overburden the child with unnecessary details. Stress the positive qualities in the new arrangement to reassure the child. Make it clear to the child that they are not to blame for the arrangement ending.

Advantages of neighbour as childminder:
• You know her
• No driving the baby each day
• Child near home, directly in her own locality
• All the advantages of Family day care (see page 35)

Disadvantages:
• Difficulty in having a business-like arrangement with a neighbour
• Embarrassing if you have to make alternative arrangements
• Child may prefer going into neighbour where all the children are rather than being in her own home

Nanny as childminder

The word 'nanny' has an old-fashioned ring about it. It replaced 'nurse' in the vocabulary of the Victorian household, which is a good thing, as the word 'nurse' implies that children are some type of illness and must be kept apart from the adults in the house, under medical supervision!

A nanny is a childminder who lives-in or comes daily to the baby's home, someone **not** related to the parents.

There is nothing old-fashioned about nannies today. Recognised and validated NNEB and City and Guilds courses are run in childcare colleges (see Appendix 3). These courses are comprehensive, covering infant care, child development, psychology, first aid, nutrition and care of the child with special needs. Practical experience in supervised placements in day nurseries is also an important component. The women have chosen childcare as a profession, which implies a love of children and having the natural flair and qualities of disposition necessary.

A live-in nanny could be a single mother, for whom live-in accommodation is an important advantage. But nannies need not necessarily be young, and some parents might feel happier to have a more mature person living in, particularly if the parents' work demands travel, with frequent overnights away from home.

Having somebody living in your home means it is her home also. She needs to have her own room, where her privacy is respected, with her own TV and perhaps also her own bathroom.

At the outset, it is important to get down on paper what the scope of the job involves and what you expect from a nanny. She will be prepared to undertake responsibility for all work in connection with the children, their meals, laundry, keeping their rooms and play areas tidy. The parents may expect a full-time housekeeping role, including shopping, cooking and cleaning. Depending on the number and ages of the children, and whether any other help is available in the household, a happy medium between these two extremes should be negotiated.

With a live-in nanny, parents go to work, leaving what seems to be a reasonably orderly house behind them. On their return in the evening, children are fed and washed and ready for bed or TV, order and calm prevail. The busy day's activities, their preparation and tidying away are not readily visible.

How to get a nanny

Before you waste your time, and a prospective nanny's time, on an interview, do the following:

- Ask for references from a previous employer and a doctor. Follow them up.
- Find out the reason for leaving the last job.
- How long did she work there? Frequent changes of employment or leaving a post as nanny at a whim are indicators of a lack of understanding of the nature of the job, and children's need for commitment and continuity of care.
- Listen carefully to the unspoken messages of previous employers, as well as to the spoken ones.
- Ask whether the nanny lived up to expectations in terms of responsibility and integrity.
- Ask if the children like her.
- Ask whether she is a good communicator.
- Ask if the previous employers know anything about her family background.
- Go through your list of the important tasks and ask how willing and able she was in these areas.
- Check if she cooks or drives.
- Check out her health and suitability for the job with the doctor's reference, as you would with a childminder.
- Be clear about what you expect from the nanny at the time of the interview.
- Define her working hours and her free time and holiday arrangements. (Remember, going on holidays with the family is not necessarily a holiday for her!)

Obviously, every single task involved will not be covered during the interview, but piling on extra responsibilities every week will not be conducive to good relations.

This might sound very prying, but before considering sharing your home and trusting somebody with your children in that private situation, you are wise and entitled to have as much information as you can.

Setting up a contract

Prepare a contract outlining the tasks included in the job, the hours, days and evenings off, payment and holiday arrangements.

Include some do's and don'ts which may be individual to you. For example:

- No slapping the children
- No alcohol in the house
- No parties in the house
- No boyfriends in the house
- Smoking confined to restricted areas in the house
- Phone calls only with permission

When making up these rules, keep in mind that your home will be her home also, and the success of the arrangement or employment depends ultimately on how 'at home' she feels in her job.

If you take an interest in her as a person and discuss her boyfriend or skin-care problems, or her family concerns in a friendly way, she will find your home a happy place to be and her sense of job-satisfaction will increase.

Human nature being what it is, it is wise to set these limits at the outset. If this nanny lives up to your highest hopes, you can relax or revise them. She may have some good friends whom you would readily welcome the odd evening. Trust will build up over time, as you get to know each other. But it is best to start with some formal rules in place and relax them as you think appropriate, than to try and introduce them in the form of sanctions, when you feel she has over-stepped the limits.

You should make a list of the 'perks' that go with the job. This may include use of a car, health insurance cover and things like family membership of sports clubs.

Allow space for her to add in her own requirements. This will reinforce for her that the relationship will inevitably be more intimate than that of an ordinary employer/employee.

The contract should be agreed with a clause allowing either parents or nanny to terminate the arrangement after three months, following a month's notice of intention. However, like any contract, when the people involved are on the same wavelength, the written contract lies buried in a drawer and is never referred to again. But if the parties are totally unsuited, by temperament, personality or failure to perform their part of the contract adequately, then no piece of paper will put things right.

The interview

Assuming you are satisfied with the references, the next step is to arrange an interiew.

The interview should take place in your home, with the children around. Everybody in the household, including family pets, should meet the prospective new family member.

How she responds to the children, by asking them questions about themselves directly, and their responses and reaction to her are obviously enormously important, but so also are the adults' feelings towards her, in the context of sharing your home with her.

Ask her about her previous work, what she liked or disliked. Has she friends nearby, or hobbies or sports which she can pursue during her time off? She will be a window onto the world and role-model for your children, and it is preferable that you are slightly constrained by her night off for swimming, badminton or night-classes than her perception of recreation consisting of six vodka-and-whites any old night!

It is healthy for her to have interests outside the home and no matter how well she fits into your family or how well you get on, it is nice to have the house to yourselves as a family. The children benefit from this special time with you. They can air their grievances, have your undivided attention, and it is a good plan to involve yourself directly with the children, story reading, or playing cards, on nanny's night off.

If she has qualifications, make enquiries about her at the college. If not, but you like her and the children like her, and she has experience, then ask if she would be interested in taking night classes. Many young girls who move away from home as nannies find this a good way of making friends with other girls in a similar situation. Her interest in studying child-care and development would be an indicator of positive motivation towards working with children.

Ask about the prospective nanny's own family background. Good parenting skills are picked up during each individual's experience as a child within the family. Has she brothers and sisters? What do they do? Are her parents living? Did she like school? Through easy conversational interaction rather than as a barrage of questions, try and build up a picture of her character and temperament.

Do not rush the interview. Read Chapter One again. Invite the prospective nanny to lunch or tea, and put her at her ease. Be natural as a family yourselves, so that she has the opportunity to get your measure also. Forget you are a prospective employer and she a would-be employee. While that is true, of course, the relationship you will have with somebody sharing your home immediately undermines formality.

Make sure that children or the baby's presence is a large part of the interview. Ideally she should show a more animated response to them than to you. Does she talk to them as people, or does she seem more anxious to impress you than the children? Go out of the room on some pretext for a while and leave her with the children to give them time to assess her.

If you seem to be getting on fine, and find her easy to talk to, don't forget to pinpoint the particular detailed needs you have. These should be written down. They may include:
• Getting children up, washed, dressed, fed in the morning
• Making up lunches
• Leaving and collecting children from school
• Making up feeds for the baby
• Running the washing machine
• Tidying up kitchen and running dishwasher
• Shopping
• Preparing vegetables for dinner
• Drying and putting away clothes
• Ironing
• Cleaning and lighting fire
• After-school meal for the children
• Homework supervision

- Cleaning shoes
- Preparing children's dinner
- Giving dinner, and clearing up afterwards
- Getting children ready for bed, baths and hairwashing
- Feeding animals
- Putting out rubbish
- Helping with adults' evening meal and clearing away
- Babysitting

This describes a very busy day and if a baby is involved as well negotiate the 'essential' activities to ensure that there is time for cuddles and playing.

If you want presses, fridges or cooker cleaned, or vacuuming and floor washing done, you must negotiate them separately from the child care duties. You might suggest that one evening or Saturday morning each month — you form a team, older children and all the adults together doing a cleaning blitz.

If the prospective nanny reacts negatively to any of the jobs — don't panic! A bit of assertiveness is a good quality. You will know where you stand, and this nanny will let you know her limits. She will be less likely to let herself become snowed under and resentful, followed by a blow-up, or a midnight flit.

The secret lies in deciding what is really important, with the children's needs taking precedence.

Assuming you are satisfied with the interviewee's training, experience, and most importantly, her references, in all, her ability to do the job, the main purpose of the interview is to try and decide will you and she and the children get on well together.

A trial run

'If you want to know me — come live with me' is an old saying. Ask her to come for a weekend, while you are at home, and this will definitely help you to be sure that she is or is not the nanny for you.

If she is still in her teens, you must take some responsibility for her, and may need to set limits on late nights, and do some gentle parenting of her. If she is under eighteen, it is a good idea to make contact with her parents, and assure them that your home is a safe place for her to be. This contact will be reassuring for her as a young person, perhaps living away from home for the first time. It will also give her an underlying message that feedom and independence from her family are not to be misinterpreted as liberty and licence.

The rates of pay for a live-in nanny vary with age, experience, qualifications, the type of accommodation and the extent of her duties. Start with a round figure of £100.00 per week. Deduct £30.00 per week for accommodation. Add on (at a rate £3.00 per hour) payment for housework not related to childcare, such as cleaning, laundry or cooking. Add on an agreed overtime payment for babysitting at £1.50 per hour. You may make deductions on the basis of perks such as use of a car during her time off. You will probably end up roughly where you started — approximately £100.00 per week.

A live-in nanny is not a cheap childcare option, but when you have the right person, and if your work involves irregular hours, working late, or over-nights away, the peace of mind is well worth the price.

Where to look

You can go about finding a nanny in a number of ways. Approach an employment agency which specialises in nannies, home-help or childminders. The agency will discuss your needs and your resources — how much you are prepared to pay, where you live, what perks your job has to offer, how many children are involved and an outline of the duties your job entails. They will send you a list of the prospective candidates and you must examine them. Select those whose particulars resemble what you have in mind, and ask the agency to get references for them. The next step is to check out the references, and then proceed to the interview stage.

Childcare colleges have graduates coming on stream each year and should be approached in April or May, when they can offer the job to the students before they disperse at the end of the course.

The National Childminding Association and various vocational colleges run courses. They can be approached any time, and may know of nannies available. (See list of useful addresses in Appendix III.)

If you work from home, or part-time, a school-leaver might meet your needs and you should contact the local secondary schools. A school-leaver might expect less payment, but where the job requires a full working week and some over-nights unsupervised, somebody very young and inexperienced might not be adequate, and might find the job too lonely or too demanding.

Remember that you will become an employer if you have a nanny, whether she comes daily, or lives in. Please read the Tax and PRSI/NI (Pay Related Social Insurance/National Insurance) section, and the note on insurance.

The wonderful advantage for your children in having a live-in nanny is the one-to-one continuous care, in their own home. Be careful not to be exploitative in terms of pay or overwork or lack of free time. Nobody likes to be exploited or unappreciated and nannies will not stay long with an unappreciative employer. If you find yourself with a succession of nannies, the children lose the advantage of continuous care from one person and you will waste time interviewing replacements and lose money paying fees to agencies.

When you find a treasure, then treasure her!

Advantages of a live-in nanny:
- Children stay in their own home
- Children have continuous care from one person
- You can select a professional, trained nanny
- She is there first thing in the morning.
- Flexibility about your coming home time, or overnights away
- A legally binding, negotiated contract exists

Disadvantages:
- Sharing your home involves a loss of privacy
- You have responsibility for nanny's welfare
- You become an employer, and must do the paperwork
- You may have a few false starts, until you find the right nanny for your family
- Heating and lighting bills run up in your home
- She will have friends and callers

Nanny live-out

Read the previous chapter on nannies. Most of the points apply to a nanny coming into your house daily. She must have the necessary skills and experience and temperament to care for the children unsupervised, in the private setting of your home.

You can find a daily nanny in the same way as seeking a live-in nanny, through the agencies, colleges or courses. But it is best to advertise locally, in supermarkets, shops, banks or post office notice boards, because it is ideal to get a nanny who lives locally. She can walk or cycle to work each morning, with less likelihood of frequent late starts. Travel to and from work is an important point to raise at the interview. Be satisfied that her plans are realistic. If she must set out at an unearthly hour to arrive in time to let you travel to work, she will be asleep by four o'clock!

The first step is to ask for references, and check them out before you interview.

Check out previous employers and work record. The same criteria apply here, as with a live-in nanny. If she lives locally, find out about her family background.

Remember, it is better to put a lot of thought and time and effort into selecting the right person, rather then subjecting yourselves and the children to a succession of 'didn't work outers'.

Take your time over the interview and make sure she sees plenty of the children, and that they interact with her during the time of the visit.

Set out the nature of the job — what you expect her to do. Describe the daily routine (see previous section) and encourage her to ask questions.

Ask her about herself. The higher her level of general education, the better, and ask if she has done any childcare courses.

Ask her to spend a day with you and the children, so you can make a final decision before she starts.

As with a live-in nanny, leave yourself an 'out' clause; two month's trial period, followed by a month's notice of intention to terminate the employment, if things are not right.

A daily nanny will not be living in your house, and you

will therefore not have the same degree of intimacy and involvement with her as you would with a live-in nanny. Nevertheless, it is important that you are on the same wavelength with her in regard to childcare practice. (Read Chapter One again.) You must be able to communicate easily with her, and trust her, but it is more important that the children like her and that she likes them, than that you would pick her as your best friend.

Make out a contract of the terms of employment, covering the following:

- Time of arrival
- Time of departure (be realistic about your working hours)
- Payment for working late
- Holidays
- An outline of the tasks involved in the job
- Rates of pay
- Phoning in before a definite time, if she is sick
- Rules of the house, as discussed in the previous chapter

Rates of pay for live-out nannies also vary considerably with age and experience. The hours involved must be taken into consideration, and a figure of £2.00 per hour could be taken as a guideline. Extra payment for staying late should be discussed and negotiated.

As with a live-in nanny, when you have the right nanny, appreciate and respect her. If she goes to aerobics on a Tuesday, make sure you are never late that evening! Remember, your ability to go out in the morning depends on her and she will obviously be better motivated towards punctuality if you are realistic and responsible about time-keeping at the other end of the day.

As in the case of childminders, parents must have a fall-back person lined up, in case the nanny is sick and to cover emergencies, such as parents working late or having to attend an urgent meeting. This ensures that no unfair pressure is put on the nanny to stay when she really cannot do so.

Nannies, as with other childminders and au pairs, work unsupervised in the private sphere of the home. Any suggestion that things are not right, from neighbours or the children, must be taken very seriously, and investigated.

Remember, your children must be safe, cared for with love and patience, and you must be able to leave the house without any doubts. Negotiate your way through breaches of the house rules, but make no concessions if the interaction with the children is brought into question. Be assertive and state clearly how you want the nanny to handle discipline or safety. If she is unwilling or incapable of responding, then you may need to make alternative arrangements.

Having a nanny coming in on a daily basis also involves you in the necessity to register as an employer, and do the necessary Tax and PRSI/NI paperwork.

Advantages of a live-out nanny as childminder:
- Children stay in their own home
- Children have continuous care from one person
- You are not sharing your home, and so retain some domestic privacy
- She may be more flexible about your coming home time than a day nursery or childminder

Disadvantages:
- You are dependent on her arrival in the mornings
- Relatively expensive option for one or two children
- Household bills running up during the day
- A fall-back person must be lined up
- You must assume the tax and PRSI/NI responsibilities as an employer

Au pair as a childminder

Au pair means 'mother's help' and refers to overseas visitors who stay with families and are prepared to help with housework and children, in exchange for a small payment and their accommodation. They are different from nannies in several respects.

An au pair's motivation is to travel, experience a different culture first-hand and learn a language. Childcare and development may not be her strong suit! If her English is poor, it is not conducive to good language development in your baby or children, and an au pair would probably be more appropriate where the children are over three years of age.

An au pair is not an employee in any sense of the word. She is a visitor to your country, who should be respected and treated as part of the family. That means eating with the adults and joining in social and sporting activities and outings if she so wishes.

Your home is her home for the duration of her stay, and like a daughter of the family, she should be able to bring her friends in occasionally. She should not expect to be confined to her room, even if you have guests, unless it is her choice.

Au pairs are usually between eighteen and twenty-four years of age so they are young adults, but because they are guests in your house and in a foreign country and in a different culture to their own, you must assume some degree of responsibility for their welfare. You should know where they are, and how they are getting home.

You are perfectly entitled to establish some house rules, like using the phone, for instance, or keeping reasonable hours and telling you where she is going during her time off. Her family will usually do the phoning at prearranged times, but sometimes she may need to ring home. If you are unwilling to have any international calls made, you can arrange to have the international dialling facility blocked at the telephone exchange.

Au pairs go to language classes, usually twice each week and these are available mornings, afternoons and evenings.

It is recommended that between three and five hours work each day is appropriate, but some are willing to care for the children during the normal weekly working hours. Make it clear to the agency when you apply for an au pair what your requirements are, so that evening classes can be arranged if a full working week is expected. Some agencies actually specialise in childcare or Montessori students and the au pairs would expect to work a full week.

Sundays are sacred, because au pairs like to meet up with their compatriots. Two half-days free, or Saturday off is expected in addition to Sundays.

An au pair will not make a clear demarcation between housework and childcare, but don't overburden her with chores. Language barriers often prohibit communication, and resentment may build up before you realise it.

Don't expect her to cook Irish food, she may not be able to. Remember the cultural difference. In comparison to continental Europe, our climate is very cold and damp, and she may not understand the necessity to air clothes properly, or she may stack up the fire when everybody is about to go to bed, and never remember the fire guard!

Take time to explain things slowly (no need to shout!) and clearly, with plenty of actual demonstrations of how things should be done. The language and cultural difference involves a longer 'getting to know each other' period than with a native nanny.

Homesickness is as real as any other form of sickness. The symptoms are crying, headaches, not eating, and staying in the bedroom. It may take a while to 'incubate' and may only appear after a week or two. It should pass in a few days, or it may appear for only a few hours at a time over a period of a few weeks. The best treatment is sympathy and consideration and kindness, and contact with other au pairs here.

Nothing disenchants an au pair as quickly as disliking the food. Bring her shopping with you and let her select food which she likes and will be able to prepare, otherwise she may take to spending her pocket money on snacks and chocolate, and then have very little left to go out and enjoy herself on her evenings off.

There are no statutory regulations about au pairs. The fate of au pairs lies in their own hands. If they do not like the treatment they receive within a family — they may simply walk out. Their agency will try to relocate them with another family, or they may have arranged to move to another family through their social network.

The rate of pay starts at £25.00 per week, where they would do a few hours housework each day probably in a household with school-going children. Their mornings would be free for language classes. They would do some babysitting, but they would expect to be free two evenings, as well as on their days off.

The pay would increase with the amount of hours worked, up to approximately £40.00 for responsibility for a full working week. The agency or language school will give you guidelines.

Au pairs are not to be treated as nineteenth-century kitchen maids, that is, as cheap slave labour. They often come from wealthy or comfortably-off families and have a high standard of education. They talk to each other and compare families and working conditions. They do not have to remain in an exploitative situation.

The principal complaints they make are not being treated as part of the host family, or that children are not corrected by parents if they are rude or discourteous to them when the parents are around.

The host families' principal complaints are that they spend hours in the bathroom and on the phone. Also, misunderstandings arise and communication is more difficult for both the adults and the children due to language barriers.

Au pairs stay for varying periods from three months to one year. Children should be made aware that the au pair will be going back to her own family eventually. Changes of care-givers sometimes set children thinking that perhaps they have done something to bring this situation about. They will accept their beloved au pair's departure, if they know at the outset that her stay is for a limited period.

Au pairs are contacted through agencies or language schools, which may charge a registration fee of between £30.00 and £45.00.

When you approach an agency or a language school, give as much detail of your requirements as they will listen to. If you need a full-time childminder, try and get someone who has experience and who is studying childcare. She will be more likely to know what to expect. The difficulty is that you take whoever comes along, without the opportunity to interview.

Ask the agency or language school what happens if things do not work out with a particular au pair. How quickly can they find an alternative placement family for her, and another for you?

Au pairs are willing to go to families outside the Dublin areas, but ensure that language classes are available. They are happy to work with single parents.

Advantages of an au pair as childminder:

- All the advantages of a live-in nanny, subject to the language classes
- Children benefit from exposure to another culture and language
- You do not become an 'employer' - liable for tax and PRSI paperwork

Disadvantages:

- No choice - you accept whoever the agency or language school sends
- Sharing your home, with some loss of privacy
- Not the ideal for children under three, but obviously with individual variation
- Language and cultural differences
- Responsibility for her health and safety
- Short duration of stay means the children have a succession of care-givers

Student live-in childminder

If you live near a third-level college, a university or regional technical college, and have a spare bedroom, you will have the option of offering accommodation to a student in exchange for babysitting and some light housework.

This is only a realistic option when children are school-going or when parents work at nights or weekends. Before you let anybody into your house, ask for references and follow them up.

Questions when considering a student live-in as childminder

- Does the student intend to go home at weekends? How long will she stay with you? Will she stay during part or all of the holidays? (Remember, the university spring holidays are not necessarily linked to Easter, and usually run for three weeks from mid-March. Summer holidays are from mid-June to early October. Christmas break is approximately three weeks.)
- Agree the tasks to be done by the student in the mornings and evenings.
- Set out your house rules.
- If you simply require babysitting in a household where the children are old enough to regulate themselves and allow the student to get on with study in a reasonably undisturbed manner, you might get rent for your spare bedroom, as well as babysitting!

You could suggest half the going rate for accommodation and specify exactly what you expect in terms of babysitting for this reduced charge. Check with the student welfare officers about the going rate for accommodation in the area. It will vary depending on whether evening meals and weekend meals are included.

When thinking about possibilities, do consider that a post graduate or mature student may be more inclined to stay in and study at nights or weekends, though not necessarily.

To find a student, ring the college and ask the student welfare office to send you an Accommodation Offered application form. Complete this and return it to the student welfare office. You can apply at any time during the academic year, and many colleges have courses and consequently accommodation needs throughout the summer also.

Advantages of a live-in student childminder:
• A second pair of hands morning and evening to help you
• Babysitting at nights
• Flexibility about coming home time for parents
• An inexpensive option
• Can be a good motivational influence on older children for study habits

Disadvantages:
• Restricted by your location
• A student is not a day care provider for young children
• Very limited amount of housework possible
• May be gone at weekends and holidays
• May lead a hectic social life
• May eat you out of home!

Day nurseries\crèches

Day nurseries or crèches are used interchangeably to describe centres for full day care for infants and pre-school children. Crèche seems to have evolved as the term for sessional care, in a shopping centre or alongside meetings, or recreational facilities. The term 'day nursery' is used here to describe a full day care facility.

State-supported day nursery provision or subsidy for places in a day care situation is limited in Ireland to where there is social or economic need. The vast majority of day nurseries, therefore, are privately owned and run, without government grants or regulations. This situation is expected to continue until 1995, when regulations concerning the standards of day care facilities for children are expected to be put in place by the Irish Department of Health.

Premises

At present, like any business, a day nursery requires planning permission. An inspection for suitability and fire safety is sometimes undertaken by the local planning authority, but this is by no means universal, and the onus of inspection is very much the responsibility of parents.

The National Children's Day Nursery Association has issued a set of guidelines, and has introduced a programme of voluntary registration. This involves an inspection of the premises, checking staff qualifications, insurance, staff-child ratio, toilet facilities and safety. Not all members of the association have applied or have been inspected for voluntary registration. Parents can obtain a list of day nurseries which are members, and which are also registered as having been inspected.

To meet the demand for day care, many privately run day nurseries have opened in cities and towns, and are listed in the Golden Pages under Schools.

Day nurseries differ from one another quite considerably. Some aim to reproduce a home environment, with emphasis on freedom and play, while others focus on early learning. Some incorporate a pre-school playgroup or formal Montessori school into the day.

Before deciding on a particular day nursery, parents should take the time to visit at least three nurseries, so as to have some basis for comparison.

Most day nurseries divide the children up by age, approximately as follows:
- Infants under one year
- Toddlers between one and two-and-a-half years
- Play-group/Montessori between two-and-a-half and five years of age

Checking out a day nursery

If considering a day nursery, get the brochures from three or four in advance, so as to avoid time wasting if some do not meet your needs, such as not taking infants.

Make an *appointment* to call and see the owner or manager, preferably during the day, while the nursery is operational.

The points you should bear in mind are:

- **Location** – the nursery should not be out of your way of travel to work.
- **Opening hours** must obviously suit parents' working hours.
- **Age** – some nurseries do not take infants, or have a minimum age requirement. Some stop at five years, others provide the full Montessori education, catering for children up to twelve years. Some provide after-school care, and will collect children from local primary schools. If older children are catered for, what activities such as sports, swimming, music, are arranged?
- **Cost** – the rates vary, depending on such factors as whether meals are provided by nursery or parents; whether a garden is available; whether pre-school play-group or Montessori school is included.
- The **person in charge** – this woman's personality will be reflected in the way things are done in the nursery. Do you like her and find her easy to talk to? Can you meet and talk to the person who will be specifically caring for your baby or child?

- **Qualifications** – certificates and diplomas are usually displayed on the wall. Make sure that the manager/supervisor and also the person who will have particular responsibility for your child, have some childcare qualifications.
- **Insurance** – if you do not see a current insurance certificate displayed, ask to see it.
- **Staff-to-child-ratio** – the following are the adult-to-child ratio recommendations of the Committee on Standards of Day Care Services for Children, (Ireland, 1985), and are a good guideline for parents:
  0 - 1 years – there should be one adult to not more than three babies.
  1 - 2 years – one adult to not more than five toddlers.
  2 years plus – one adult to six children.
  Many nurseries operate with higher children-to-adult ratios than these recommendations suggest.
- **Space** - Does the nursery look overcrowded? 2.32 square metres per child is recommended. Overcrowding has implications for child development as well as for safety in everyday routine. Overcrowding obviously hinders evacuation in the event of an emergency.
- **Outdoor play** is a very normal part of a day's activity, but not all nurseries have access to a garden. Walks and outings to parks are substituted. Check if the garden is safe for the children and secure against intruders.
- **Indoor play** - Are there enough toys and books to go around, and sufficient variety in these? Are the staff interacting with the children, talking to them and encouraging them to use the toys available, rather than standing and watching?
- **Meals** - Are they provided, cooked daily in the nursery? A typical weekly menu should be available. Most nurseries provide a cooked meal and two snacks. Sometimes the children bring their preferred snacks, but this varies from nursery to nursery.
- **First Aid** - A trained member of staff should be on hand at all times. A nursery should be equipped with a well-stocked first aid box.
- **Safety** - Central heating is a necessity and no open fires or naked flame heaters should be used. Radiators should have guards fitted.

- The rooms should be bright, warm, and well ventilated.
- **Windows** should have safety bars at child level, but should be potential emergency exits.
- **Stairs** should have safety gates at top and bottom.
- **Fire** extinguishers and smoke detectors should be visible.
- Bearing in mind the number of adults and children, and looking at the size and layout of the nursery, parents should consider if evacuation is a realistic possibility in the event of an emergency.
- **Hallways** or stairways should not be constricted by coat rails, bags or buggies. These should be stored out of circulating space.
- **Floor coverings** should not be worn or torn.
- Children should not have access to the kitchen.
- **Toilets** - there should be one toilet and wash hand basin for every ten children over two. Staff should have separate toilet facilities.
- **Structure of the day** - Parents should have some idea of how their child will spend the day. There should be plenty of time and space for free play, running, climbing, tricycles, tractors, pushing and pulling toys. There should also be a quiet place for reading or concentrated work for older children.
- **Staff turnover** - A high staff turnover has implications of an over-regulated atmosphere. Children will not be happy with stressed staff. Most nurseries take students for practical experience placement purposes. This practice has the beneficial effect of increasing the adult-to-child ratio, but it is important that children know that the staff are permanent. They can then readily accept the coming and going of students. A high staff turnover, along with students on temporary placements, is not good for children.
- If leaving a baby in a day nursery, your focus of interest will be the **baby room.** It should not be too crowded and there should be walking space between cots. It should be warm but well ventilated. If there are more than three babies to each care-giver, the feeding and changing will leave little time for cuddling and playing.

Ask which one person will care for your baby continuously. Talk to her and ask to spend some time with her. It is unfair her. It is unfair to have somebody peering over one's shoulder during the course of the day's work, in any situation, but you must be certain that your baby is in loving, patient and capable hands. A good baby care-giver will understand your needs.

• **Hygiene standards**

— Is there a sink with hot water for hand washing? A high standard of hygiene is required to prevent infection spreading among babies. Each should have her own cot, feeding and toilet requisites, marked with the child's name. Cot linen should be changed daily, more often if necessary.

— Is the changing table well away from where bottles or food are left? Are the care-givers themselves scrupulously clean in the matter of hair, clothes and fingernails?

— Indoor shoes should be used in the baby room. The floor should not be carpeted, it should be washable and clean, but not have a slippery surface.

— There should be a comfortable chair for each care-giver, or they will be less inclined to sit and play with babies.

- The baby room is the one room where order, cleanliness and tidiness are evident. There should be a place for everything, and everything in its place, leaving floors uncluttered.

— Pictures and mobiles should be plentiful.

However, infants grow and you should look at all areas of the nursery while you are there.

While parents can satisfy themselves about suitability on the basis of the tangible criteria outlined, the really important mothering qualities are less easily observed and evaluated. Your presence as an observer for even a few minutes interferes with the very interaction process which you wish to observe. The children stop doing their usual activities to find out about you, and the staff may become self-conscious, for example, about sitting on the floor and playing at the children's level.

Notice how the care-givers respond to the situation. Children should not be over-regimented and their curiosity about a stranger in their environment should be perfectly acceptable. The outgoing children will come forward to tell you who they are, to find out all about you. The care-giver should be watching for the response from the more timid children. One or more children may feel uneasy about a stranger arriving to look at them. Some may even make strange and cry, and be waiting for reassurance from their familiar care-giver that you are okay.

Watch the children for a few minutes and see if any are just sitting about, not involved with play material, or interacting with other children, and observe how responsive the care-givers are to this. All children need attention, and sometimes the more outgoing children succeed naturally in getting it, to the disadvantage of the quieter ones. The sensitive care-giver will keep an eye on all the children, integrating those who need encouragement and talking and chatting and intervening where necessary to ensure that each child's need for interaction and stimulation are met.

If the care-givers are standing together, chatting to each other, with one ear on the radio, and merely keeping an eye out to avert trouble or respond to it, that is not a good sign.

Kneel down to get a child's-eye view of the surroundings. Do the rooms look very crowded? Can you see out the window from this level? Remember that a child in full day care needs the environment to be as rich and stimulating as possible. The day nursery and its staff are the children's window onto the world and must offer much more than a place of safe containment.

- **Play**
  - The walls should display plenty of evidence of the children's art and craft work and there should be wall charts of natural history, maps and interesting posters or paintings.
  - Look out for photographs of trips to the zoo, the beach, the woods, picnics, and ask if such trips are arranged. Day nursery insurance usually covers such trips, provided the adult-to-child ratio is adequate.
  - Musical instruments are a good sign, because children learn language and co-ordination from singing and dancing.
  - Look at the toys and equipment such as tables and chairs. They should not be broken or dirty. Books should be plentiful — even pre-language children love having stories read. There should be plenty of shelving at

children's level so that they can have ready access to books and toys, without having to ask.

— It is reasonable to see a television and video in a day nursery, but ask how many hours viewing is allowed during the course of the day, and balance that with the time it occupies at home.

— Plenty of cushions or bean bags are a sign that toddlers can be comfortable while reading or just relaxing, maybe with a bottle, without being put into a cot to sleep.

— Listen to the noise level. Floor and ceiling finishes, curtains and furniture should be sound-absorbent, so that neither children nor care-givers need to shout continuously.

— Parents should spend long enough in the prospective nursery to observe good interaction and should not feel that they are a nuisance. Visits from prospective parents are all part of a week's work, even in a busy day nursery. But parents should be reasonable. Study the brochure well in advance of the visit, so as not to waste time asking questions already answered in it. Don't accept an offer of tea or coffee - it wastes good observation time, because you cannot wander about a nursery with a hot drink in your hand.

Remember to treat staff with the courtesy you would give any other professional providing a service. Especially bear in mind the fact that your relationship with these care-givers is important for your child's development. It is a far more open and intimate one, requiring greater ease of communication than would be expected with teachers, doctors or dentists. Be aware that the children have priority in a good day nursery, which they see as their home-from-home. You should be ready for the probability of your guided tour being interrupted. Allow an hour to make an informed decision.

• **Money**

— A deposit of a weekly or monthly payment in advance is sought at the time of booking. A list of conditions or procedures not covered in the marketing brochure is usually available. It is best to take these away and study them before committing yourself. You should be clear on the following points:

— Charges - in advance? The daily, weekly or monthly rate? How payable, by cash, cheque? Charges for late collection? Full or partial charges for when child is sick or otherwise not in attendance? Reduction for subsequent children?

— If Montessori or pre-school playgroup are involved, do these constitute an additional charge?

— Days, holidays, during which the nursery is closed?

— Freedom of access for parents to call?

— Procedures regarding sickness and dispensing of medication?

A form requesting information about your child will be given to parents for completion which you should take away and complete carefully and legibly, preferably typed, and make a note to update the information at three monthly intervals in your diary, and do so if necessary. (See Appendix II for details.)

• **Contract**

A contract will be offered, usually setting out the fee arrangements, refundability or otherwise of deposits, and undertaking to accept the conditions and procedures, late collection fines, notice required or fee payment in lieu, in the event of removing a child, and permission to give specified medication. (See Appendix I for details.)

• **Contact**

If a formal structure for communication between parents and the care-giver outside delivery/collection times is not referred to, ask what the usual procedure is. Parents should be able to talk, at least on a monthly basis, free from interruption, to the care-giver principally involved with the child. This enables either party to raise matters which are a cause of concern, in a non-threatening way.

Talk to other parents who use the day nursery. Word of mouth recommendation from somebody you know is invaluable.

Getting settled

When bringing your baby for the first time, make sure that

she is awake and settled before you leave, and be prepared to spend as long as is required to ensure this.

Settling in a toddler or older child is best done gradually. One parent should bring the child and stay in the nursery with the child for a limited period on the first day. On the second visit the parent should stay for a shorter time and leave the child for a little while and so on. The purpose of this is to build up confidence in the child to trust the new environment and trust the parent to come back and collect her at the promised time. It is recommended that this process goes on over a period of a week, before a parent returns to work. Day nurseries obviously want children to settle in happily, and many do not charge for the sessions during the settling-in period.

The parent should not become involved in play activity — that should be left to the staff. The child will be more reluctant to let the playmate/parent leave! The parent should rather sit quietly at the side of the room, allowing the child freedom to join in play or be near the parent.

The parent should show particular warmth and friendliness towards the care-giver who will be involved with the child. Children pick up tension intuitively, and parents must act happy, even though they are experiencing some tugs at their heartstrings.

Bribes and treats for the child should be avoided, because they convey the impression to the child that attending day nursery is some form of unpleasant duty. The child should become motivated by the possibility of playmates, toys and activities, outings and birthday parties in the day nursery, as rewards in themselves.

Day nursery staff are experienced in settling in new children, and parents should listen to their suggestions. Parents should also listen carefully to their children if they are trying to relate something they don't like. It may be something which could quite readily be put right, like bringing a comfort blanket or soother along.

A toddler or older child may be happy to stay in a day nursery as long as a parent also stays there, and protest when the parent starts to leave. Promise truthfully that you will be back at a certain time and stick to that promise. It is a difficult time for both parent and child and skilled nursery staff understand this and help to ease the child in and the parent out! Parents should be contactable by telephone and free to come and comfort a child who is unable to settle. Trying to sneak off while the child is temporarily distracted is bad practice because it obviously undermines the child's trust in the parent, and will not be helpful in building up a trusting relationship with the care-giver. A good care-giver will not recommend this to a parent.

Day nurseries cost approximately £55.00 per week, but there may be an additional charge as children get older and Montessori school until 2.00 pm is included.

Advantages of a day nursery for your child:
• Children become socialised
• The day is structured
• Variety in activities provided
• Less expensive than one-to-one care

Disadvantages:
• Continuous care from one care-giver is generally not available
• Lack of subsidy or tax relief to parents often results in overcrowding in order to make the service economically viable
• Location generally involves removing children from their locality

Workplace day nurseries\crèche

Some companies have made space available for the provision of a day nursery. Very often, the running of the nursery is franchised to somebody not employed by the company. Therefore, they should be assessed by parents in the same way as privately-run day nurseries are. (See pages 72-78).

Obviously, parents who use the workplace nursery are colleagues who know each other and can come together to have a say in the standards to which it operates, and can ensure that it meets their needs.

Parents feel that they are close at hand and can spend lunchtime with their children. Such proximity makes breast-feeding a realistic possibility for nursing mothers.

But it may not be possible or reasonable to spend each lunchtime or coffee break in the nursery. While in theory day nursery staff welcome parents, the reality means that the routine is disturbed, and the child may expect to go home when the parent is returning to work for the afternoon. This may be unsettling for the child. Children whose parents cannot visit during the day may feel resentful.

Parents must use common sense and follow their instincts. They should try not to feel guilty about disturbing the nursery routine by visiting, or guilty about not visiting the nursery during the day.

If they enjoy being with the child, going for a walk with them or feeding a baby, then the child will enjoy it too, and even a busy nursery must accommodate parents' needs as well as children's.

If shopping or appointments make visiting an occasional treat, then the child will accept and welcome them. Guilt is a negative emotion, and may lead parents into making promises which are impossible to fulfil, or to blurring the difference between a treat and a bribe.

Parents should check if they can use the workplace nursery if they are on holidays or leave-of-absence from work.

If the parent is sick, it is not always possible to get the child to the nursery and parents should be clear about what the fee arrangements are in this case and have a stand-by arrangement for such emergencies.

Workplace nurseries may be subsidised by the company.

Advantages of a workplace nursery:
- As for day nurseries in general
- Parents can have a say in how it is run
- Proximity allows for contact at lunchtime
- No extra travel involved

Disadvantages:
- As for day nurseries in general
- Some parents find they feel guilty if they don't call to see their children during a break.
- If parent is sick/absent from work — child will need to go somewhere — make emergency arrangements.

Pre-school playgroups and *Naíonraí* (Irish-speaking playgroups)

Pre-school playgroups cater for thousands of children from three to five years of age. Children vary in their readiness to go to playgroup. When signs of boredom with household activities appear, and when the face lights up on the arrival of a playmate, then perhaps the time has come to go to playgroup. Most pre-school playgroups use the criterion of being toilet-trained before they will accept the child. This is obviously in the child's interests as well as in the playgroup leader's. Pre-school playgroups are incorporated into the routine in many day nurseries.

The emphasis in the playgroups is on play and learning through play, with no suggestion of lessons. Activities include play-dough, water play, sand play, painting, jigsaws, dance and music, nature study, arts and crafts, and use educational toys to encourage problem-solving and dexterity. Most provide the opportunity for outdoor play also.

Community playgroups exist, but usually depend on an input from parents on a rota basis, or require help with outings, and consequently the charges are less, but working parents may not be available to become involved.

The Irish Pre-School Playgroups Association (IPPA) runs courses and sets out guidelines and a code of standards, which cover such points as space, indoor and outdoor play areas, equipment, washing and toilet facilities, health, safety and hygiene.

The IPPA recommends that the number of children should not exceed twenty in any one group, with an adult-to-child ratio of one adult to eight children. It is also recommended that the playgroup leader be there continually, with a rota basis acceptable for the helpers.

Many insurance policies for playgroups insist on two adults being present all the time.

The IPPA can provide a list of playgroups which are registered with the association, and they have four advisors who are regionally based, and who visit playgroups which are members of the association.

Playgroups usually operate between 9.30 am and 12.30 pm and may not be suitable for working parents unless integrated with another form of childcare to deliver and collect the children.

The cost of having a child in a playgroup is approximately £15.00 per week.

Naíonraí, or Irish-speaking playgroups, originally developed under the auspices of Conradh na Gaeilge and are now encouraged and regulated by An Comhchoiste Réamhscolaíochta. There are over two hundred now in existence. They cater for almost 2,500 children between three years and school-going age. They operate in parish halls, community centres, schoolrooms or in private houses.

The children come together for two or three hours each day, in a pleasant environment, under the guidance of a *stiúrthóir* or supervisor, to play and learn through play. In common with all pre-school playgroups, the environment is structured to ensure that all facets of the child's development are catered for, while at the same time giving them the opportunity of acquiring the Irish language naturally. It is stressed that Irish is acquired naturally, through play, and not through formal lessons or teaching.

Some preliminary work is done in *naíonraí* on the development of skills involved in reading, writing and mathematics. The supervisor uses Irish, along with action rhymes and songs to help make the words and phrases self-explanatory. The recommended ratio is one adult to eight children. Parents are always welcome. There is no pressure on the children to speak Irish, but it is obviously important to the children, and vital to the success of the *naíonra*, that parents are well disposed to the Irish language, even if not fluent speakers themselves.

There is no basis for parents fearing that a child's English would suffer by exposure to a second language. Many children throughout the world speak one language at home and encounter a different language at school, and cope without difficulty. Children acquire this second language easily at this age, in the same way in which they learn the first language, by listening, interaction, understanding, isolating words and structure and eventually producing phrases and sentences themselves. The first language is not lost or diminished. In fact, the total language ability is promoted.

Amazingly, bilingual children have no difficulty in separating one language from another. The ease of acquiring more than one language during the language acquisition phase (from birth to five years, principally) does not resemble the effort required by an adult to learn another language.

The national body, An Comhchoiste Réamhscoilaíochta, runs the training courses and in-service training for supervisors. The body operates a group insurance scheme, so all *naionraí* are insured. Appropriate audio and video tapes, books, wall charts and other learning materials are prepared and disseminated by the body.

Like IPPA, its representatives attend seminars and workshops organised by Barnardo's, OMEP (World Organisation for Early Childhood Education), and others concerned with child development. The *stiúrthóirí* are therefore well informed on current trends in early child development, and are not elitist or isolated.

The cost to have a child in a *naionra* is approximately £10.00 per week.

Children have been shown to benefit from attending preschool playgroups. They show a stronger commitment to learning and doing well in school. They achieve higher scores in reading, arithmetic and language tests at all grades. They display a better orientation to work.

Advantages of a pre-school playgroup:
- Pre-schooling has been shown to give long-term educational advantages
- Children benefit from learning through play and organised interaction with other children
- Children are better prepared for 'big school'
- They provide a child with the opportunity to experience a far wider range of play materials and books than would be available at home
- Pre-school playgroups are widely available and are integrated into most day nurseries

Disadvantages:
- They start too late in the mornings for most working parents
- Collection and afternoon care is required.

Montessori

These schools take their name from Dr Maria Montessori, who opened a house for underprivileged children in Rome early this century. From her observation of children and her study of philosophy, psychology and anthropology, she understood that children, even unruly children, become readily absorbed in purposeful activities. The key is to provide each child with experiences and problems which are exactly appropriate to that particular child's stage of development.

The environment must be absolutely geared to the needs of the children, where they gain experience through activity and movement, as well as absorbing information through using specially designed equipment.

The equipment provides concrete experiences through which the child learns to become a trained observer, to compare size, shape and numbers. The material is designed to enable children to correct their own mistakes.

The role of the Montessori teacher is not that of a regular teacher, imparting knowledge to the child in the traditional sense. Instead it is to guide each child's progress, at their own pace. The child makes the choice about what material to work with and takes responsibility for that material and puts it back carefully when the task is finished. Great respect is shown for the material.

The children have freedom to move about and work with equipment suitable for their stage. But each child is aware of being a member of a group and learns that individual freedom should not impinge on the freedom of the other children, who are also entitled to work undisturbed. There is also group work and activities.

The method encourages the development of independence, decision-making, consideration for others and acceptance of personal responsibility. The aim is to help the child discover that problem-solving and learning brings its own reward, and to foster learning and reasoning skills which become a lifelong resource.

Parents should read one of Dr Montessori's books, so as to understand how their children are learning or some may be inclined to feel that their child is not making adequate progress. Dr Montessori considered the child's whole environment, both at home and at school, to be significant. Parents should also attend a session at the school, where the material and philosophy are explained. They should try and guard against asking the child 'What did you do at school today?' The child may not understand the significance of the work done and the knowledge absorbed through it, or may not have the language to describe it.

Children start Montessori school at about three and the system and equipment designed by Dr Montessori caters for children up to twelve, or comparable to the primary school cycle. But very few Montessori schools cater for children above the age of five. Where they do, it is necessarily an expensive option, but includes preparation for entrance examinations to secondary schools.

Many day nurseries incorporate Montessori school into the programme. Parents should note that there ought to be adequate space for children to move about freely and to spread mats on the floor, in order to create individual work space. The ideal ratio is one Montessori teacher to eight children.

Parents should be satisfied that the teacher holds a Diploma in Montessori Education and could contact the college or body which issues the diploma to ascertain that the school meets the requirements to provide a formal Montessori education.

Parents sometimes worry whether children will have difficulties adjusting to 'big school' after the experience of the more personally-orientated Montessori setting. The answer is they will have no more difficulty in adjusting than any child, but they will come to school eager and able to learn, with a well-developed sense of self, and be more likely to seek out additional knowledge for themselves.

Fees are approximately £650.00 per year per child, rising to approximately £750.00 per year when the children are older and the school day is longer. They may be payable monthly, or in two instalments, in September and February.

Advantages of Montessori schools:
- They teach children how to learn and reason
- Each child learns at her own pace
- They promote the development of the whole person
- The underlying philosophy promotes self-esteem and

respect for others and for the environment

Disadvantages:
- Can be expensive
- May be only for 2/3 hours — not full day care
- The system requires a child-centred attitude at home to be effective
- Parents must understand how the learning process occurs
- The system is designed to continue until age twelve for the full benefit to be achieved but most children move into ordinary schools at a much earlier age

After-school care

By five years of age, the child will usually go to school from 9 am until 1.30 pm and by seven, she will stay at school until 2.30 pm and afternoon care only is required.

At secondary school age, from about twelve onwards, parents complain that their children really need a chauffeur to ferry them from school to activities and home again, rather than childcare. You may need to be collector-driver on your way home from work, or do the Saturday football or hockey runs, in exchange for chauffeuring by other parents during the week.

As long as children are at school, you must make them answerable for their movements, whether to a neighbour, or by arrangement, to a friend's parents. Avoid leaving your house unlocked and unsupervised, no matter how trustworthy and sensible your own children are. The fact will soon become known and your house will become the gathering place in the neighbourhood, possibly beyond the limit-setting ability of your children. If anything happens to a child in your home, you are responsible.

As the children get older, discuss the day care arrangements with them and listen carefully to their needs and choices. Don't leave them in a situation where their freedom is too restricted, or without accountability for their whereabouts.

Whether children are starting in a new school, or moving up a year, the autumn after-school care should be planned during the Easter/summer term. Go to the school and enquire about swimming sessions, sports, music lessons, or extra curricular language, dance or drama classes or scouts. Find out what days and at what time they take place. School-based after-school activities make life simple.

Discuss such options with the children, and, obviously, do not try to force them to participate in activities which don't appeal to them.

Look at the notice boards in the locality, because, to meet the demand for after-school care, arts and crafts, drama, or similar activities are often advertised. You may contact a childminder there, who is offering after-school care in her home or in yours.

When you have decided what activities your children are interested in, work out what your childminding requirements are. Children at primary school should be collected after school and you may consider doing a morning to-school run, in exchange for the to-home-after-school run. You may decide to move from a full day care-giver to an afternoon housekeeper who would come to your home on non-activity afternoons. She would collect the children and bring them home, and prepare the evening meal, or do ironing, while the children get started on homework.

School holidays, church holidays and parent-teacher meetings, as well as unexpected days off school, must also be planned for. Casual arrangements with friends' parents are fine for the unexpected days off or church holidays. But put them on either a barter or financial footing, when making school-holiday arrangements.

When children reach twelve or thirteen, you can consider a month in the Gaeltacht or an exchange with a continental European child of a similar age. The disadvantage of such exchanges is that the quality of your holiday period as a family may be diminished by having to encompass the needs of the visitor.

Summer camps, live-in or on a daily basis, are run in many schools at primary and secondary level. Advertisements appear in the newspapers around Easter. They are not a cheap form of summer care, and usually occupy two or three weeks.

But the summer holidays are long, just over two months in primary schools, and three months in secondary school. An au pair for a three-month period might suit best (See au pair section). Third level students are motivated by travel and money, and are not generally an option for summer holiday childcare provision. A local teenager might fill in for church holidays and Easter and Christmas holidays, but might not be adequate to the task of regulating older children for a three-month period.

Children's opinions about their day care arrangements and their care-giver should be given careful attention from the time they can talk. As they develop from seven or eight onwards, they will express clear preferences for where they would like to be after school. They might be home-birds and resent not being at home, or may prefer one friend's house to another. Try and accommodate their wishes, as far as is practicable. Parents have found themselves paying a childminder and later finding out, to their embarrassment, that their children have spent most afternoons in another child's home nearby.

Whatever after-school arrangements you make for older children, establish at the outset with the children and the care-giver that homework must be tackled. Be prepared to spend some time after the evening meal checking that it is done, looking out for notes or comments from teachers and if necessary explaining and helping where the child has difficulties.

At primary school, the child has one teacher for all subjects, and so the parent/teacher meeting is a matter of an hour or so. At secondary school, parent/teacher meetings (at which the children may end up with one, two, or even three days off school,) require a morning or afternoon set aside. You must queue to see each of your child's (or children's) teachers and this can mean eight or nine individual interviews! Obviously, both parents can get through the session in half the time. But, as with school concerts and plays, swimming galas and sports days, you would be unwise, as parents, to miss them.

Teachers, being human, may lose interest in a child's progress, if they perceive the parents to be lacking in interest. If difficulties arise in school such as homework not being done satisfactorily, or bullying or withdrawn behaviour appearing, it helps to be able to approach a teacher whom you have already met.

From the children's viewpoint, their teachers play a large part in their life experience and they will not be able to talk intelligently to you in either positive or negative terms, if you have no idea of the person talked about.

As children get older and examinations loom, a group of like-minded parents could approach the school and request after-school supervised study. Some of the parents might be prepared to do the supervision, with a contribution from all parents providing the remuneration. Schools may need to extend their insurance cover, and may wish to be paid for heat and light. It is up to the parents to whip up enough enthusiasm to make it viable. The more students involved, the less resistance they will offer. But all work and no play is not recommended, and a balance between after-school sports, activities and supervised study is obviously to be negotiated.

Although it is a problem to keep all the considerations in mind, try not to give the impression that the children are some kind of inconvenience, or that they are paper parcels to be dropped off or collected at will. They may well take the lead by suggesting a household where you could approach the parents to make an after-school arrangement. If you discuss the possibilities with your children, you will remove their feelings of powerlessness, even though children know that they must accede to practical considerations, and ultimately to your wishes in the long run.

Childcare for children with special needs

Parents of children with special needs are encouraged, as far as possible, to integrate their children into society. Most children with special needs have more in common with normally developing children than is commonly believed. They share the need to explore the environment, to become as mobile and dextrous as possible, to play, have friends, solve problems and attend to their personal needs.

The difficulties experienced by parents in finding quality day care increase when children have special needs. When a day care provider is approached by parents of a child with special needs, the focus of attention centres on how caring for this child will affect the running of the day care facility and how it will impact on other children cared for. This focus has the effect of overshadowing the perfectly normal needs of childhood.

The criteria which apply when deciding on childcare for children with special needs are just like those of other children; the child's needs must be met. Children with visual or hearing impairment, asthma, epilepsy, Down's syndrome or mild mental handicap, to name but a few, are capable of benefiting from integration into the pre-school playgroup or Montessori school environment.

As is the case when considering any childcare provision, the quality of the person, the number of children being cared for, the space and facilities available, will all be factors which parents must consider when looking for a suitable place for their child. Parents should be careful not to be so overcome with gratitude when they find day care which accepts children with special needs that they become reluctant to monitor the quality of care in a critical way.

Staff qualifications are important in ensuring that the child's particular difficulties are understood. Dietary needs and special exercises for motor and manipulative dexterity, or speech therapy should be within the scope of ordinary day care provision.

Where a child would not benefit from sharing a care-giver within the context of a busy day nursery setting, parents could consider a care-giver coming into the home.

Courses for specialised day care are run in centres caring for children with special needs. Parents should contact the Director of Community Care in their local area for information about special day care units in the area, where specially trained students could be contacted.

In countries like the UK, where childminders are registered, trained and supervised, public health authorities frequently use selected childminders to care for children with special needs. In Ireland the parents would have to undertake finding a suitably experienced childminder, and could start by enquiring at the local health centre.

It is beyond the scope of this guide to consider the individual areas where children have special needs, and parents could be misled into believing that day care provision is readily available. This is not the case and the burden of lobbying for resources to be allocated to meet these needs, as well as fundraising, falls heavily on to parents. Places in day care and residential units are insufficient for the demand.

The characteristics of good day care provision for children with special needs can be identified as follows:

- A strong, innovative local leader (who may be a parent), who is aware that the need exists and is determined to organise an appropriate day care facility to meet that need, is very important.
- That leader is joined by families who desperately need the service.
- The facility which introduces special day care will usually already be providing high quality day care, which makes them open to recognising the importance of every child's need for love, play, interaction and autonomy.
- The director and staff of such a centre are usually highly motivated to have a positive attitude towards integration of children with special needs, wherever possible.
- They are usually willing to incorporate visits from specialised therapists into the daily routine, and provide the necessary space and facilities.

A list of voluntary associations is given in Appendix III (pages 135-139) and parents should contact the relevant voluntary body for advice and support.

The National Rehabilitation Board published a directory

of Day Care and Day Activity Centres for adults and children with disabilities, categorised by local area, and by type of disability.

When parents are trying to identify a child's special needs, with a view to full day care, it may be helpful to keep the following points in mind:

- Day care should be responsive to each individual child's ability and rigid labelling should be avoided as far as possible.
- Children should not be denied a place in a day care facility with other children, just because they have special needs, unless the child would be unsafe or would not benefit in any way from an ordinary day care setting.
- The day care facility must welcome the assistance of professionals, on a sessional basis, to meet special needs, and ordinary day care staff should be trained, where necessary, to provide for a child's special needs.
- Community resources should be sought by parents and care-givers, and integrated into the day care.
- Coming into contact with children who share the needs of all children, but who have additional needs as well, enriches the experience of all the children in any day care setting

Insurance

Whichever day care option you decide to use, insurance cover should be investigated.

If using a day nursery, workplace nursery, pre-school playgroup or Montessori school, check that they carry insurance cover against any accident which could happen to your child, as a result of negligence on the part of the owner, employees or placement students. The cover should be up to one million pounds.

The cost of cover starts at approximately £140.00 per year for up to fourteen children, and increases with the number of children involved. The policy stipulates an adult-to-child ratio of one to seven, with a minimum of two adults in attendance.

If you leave your baby with a childminder, she should be insured also. The cost for cover for up to three minded children is approximately £125.00 per year.

A nanny, minder or au pair coming into your home to care for children there may be insured by the third-party liability cover included in your own household policy. Check this with your insurance company or broker. What this means is that you will be insured against any claim for compensation by her for any injury she may sustain as a result of negligence on your part. She is unlikely to carry insurance cover to protect herself against any claim which might arise from her negligence in relation to the child or children. You could consider taking out such cover, which would cost approximately £130.00 per year.

Having such cover would ensure that your child or children would be able to recover damages if they were injured through her negligence.

Contact an insurance company or broker, and read the small print. Shop around among those who do provide this type of cover.

Becoming an employer - tax and PRSI/NI (National Insurance)

Having a nanny, either living-in or coming daily, you become an employer and must register with your local tax office, or contact the National Employer Control Section of the Inland Revenue Department.

Apply for an Employers' Registration Form and return it to the tax office. They will then send you a registration number, and the address of whichever tax office you will deal with.

Your nanny will give you a P.45 Form, if she has been in employment previously. If not, she must get a Form 12 or 12A from any tax office, and complete it. She will then receive a P.45. You, as employer, must fill in the bottom half of Page 3 of the P.45 and return it to the Tax Office. You will be sent a Tax Deduction Card and a Certificate of Tax-Free Allowance for the nanny.

You must make the necessary deductions, and use a P.30 Form to make monthly payments to cover Tax and PRSI/NI contributions to the appropriate tax office. You may make the payments at four-monthly or six-monthly intervals, if you prefer.

If the person employed by you is earning less than a taxable income, the obligation to make PRSI/NI contributions still rests with you, and you follow the procedure set out above. This is not complicated and it is very important that you take your responsibility as an employer seriously. These are statutory requirements, and failure to comply leaves you open to prosecution.

From the nanny's point of view, having Tax and PRSI/NI paid up to date enables her to claim entitlements such as optical, dental and unemployment benefits. A person earning less than £79.00 per week (with a further £12.00 if travel to work is involved) is entitled to apply for a medical card. The initial enquiry in this regard can be made through the Eastern Health Board's Freephone information service - dial 1800 520 520. National Health cover (NI) is available to all in UK.

Detailed information about your particular situation can be had from the Employer Control Section of the Inland Revenue, Lyon House, Upper O'Connell Street, Dublin 1

3

Is the childcare really working?

A child's growth and development should be a continuous process. Babies vary enormously in size, rate of growth, and in the age at which they walk and talk.

It is very important, and not always easy for working parents, to bring the baby to the public health clinic for developmental assessment and vaccinations at the appropriate ages. Obviously such clinics see babies and young children all the time and are in a position to reassure you that your baby's progress is normal, no matter how different it is to your friend's baby or your nieces or to the developmental pattern of your other children. If there is something wrong, it should be picked up at the appropriate time and remedial action taken sooner rather than later.

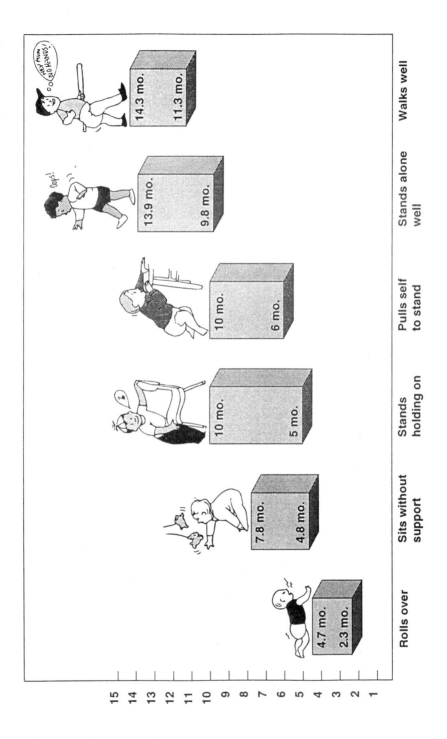

The chart on page 100 shows the wide span during which it is normal for baby to achieve certain milestones. As a guide for you to ensure that your child is developing, even though you are not with her all day — check for the following signs:

By 12 weeks, babies should:
• Look promptly at a toy dangled in front of them
• Follow visually the movement of a toy moved in a semicircle in front
• Bob head forward when held sitting, but will be held steady at forty-five degrees when on tummy on a flat surface
• Hold hands open or closed loosely
• Hold a toy which is put into hand with an active grasp
• Coo and chuckle
• 'Talk' back if you nod head and talk to them
• Hold up and look at their own hands
• Pull at clothes.

By 16 weeks, babies should:
• Wave arms and move body at sight of toy dangled if on back, or put on table, if held in sitting position
• Look at a toy in their hand
• Take a toy to mouth, when lying on their back
• Head steady, set forward, when held sitting
• Hold head at ninety degrees when on tummy
• Scratch, finger and clutch at clothes
• Bring hands together at mid-line and play with their own fingers
• Laugh out loud
• Get excited, breathe heavily, in play
• Start to smile when people just come and stand beside them
• Recognise bottle, just on sight.

By 20 weeks, babies should:
• Bring both hands up towards toy, on back, or if held in a sitting position
• Grasp toy if held approximately an inch away from their hand
• Look after a toy dropped within sight
• Hold their head erect when held sitting
• Push whole chest up when on tummy

- Scratch on tabletop when held sitting or on blanket, if on tummy
- Squeal like a piglet, voice up high
- Smile at self if held close to a mirror
- Put both hands on bottle when feeding.

By 24 weeks, babies should:
- Reach and pick up or take a toy with both hands
- Reach for toy dropped within reach
- Put toy in mouth when held supported sitting
- Grasp foot when lying on back
- Roll on the tummy and get both arms out from under chest
- Pick up a small toy and hold in centre of palm clasping with all fingers
- Grunt and growl making deep sounds
- Initiate 'conversation' with toys or people
- Know strangers from family
- Smile and talk to themselves if held close to a mirror.

By 28 weeks, babies should:
- Reach and pick up or take a toy with one hand only
- Transfer a toy easily from hand to hand
- Bang a toy up and down when held sitting
- Lift head up when lying on their back
- Sit, if put on hard surface, leaning on hands
- Stand, if chest held under arms
- Pick up a small toy and hold to palm of hand with second and third fingers
- Put whole hand on a crumb and 'rake' it
- Say 'Mum-mum-mum' especially when crying
- Make some vowel sounds in series 'ah-ah-ah, uh-uh-uh, oh-oh-oh'
- Feet to mouth when lying on back
- Reach out and pat self in the mirror.

By 32 weeks babies should:
- Pick up one small toy and then a second one
- Hold these two toys for a length of time
- If given a string with a toy attached, should pull string upwards, towards them, to get the toy
- Sit for one minute on a hard surface
- Stand, hands held shoulder height

- Pivot in a circle, using arms, when on tummy, on a hard surface
- Try to pick up a crumb by raking with thumb, second and third fingers, usually with little arm movement
- Make single consonant sounds, 'da, ba, ga, ka'
- Bite and chew toys, not just licking
- Persist in trying to reach for toys out of reach.

By 36 weeks babies should:
- Drop one of two toys picked up, to take a third one offered
- Hit toy on table with the toy in their hand
- Hold toy in one hand and play with a toy attached to a string in the other hand
- Sit for over ten minutes on a hard surface
- Stand against furniture if put there, and not lean against it
- Pick up small toy in between ends of fingers
- Pick up a crumb, using thumb and index finger
- Say 'da da, ba ba' - without meaning
- Imitate cough, or tongue click
- Know their own name
- Hold own bottle, pick it up if dropped, and finish it
- Feed themselves a biscuit, and do a good job.

These are milestones which describe the stage of development reached by most children at each age. But some children may do some things earlier or later than when described. It is not suggested that you test your baby every month, but it is important to notice that they are making continuous progress and it is very exciting to observe new abilities.

4

If things go wrong

Every baby is an individual, and no blueprint handbook of
perfect practice will suit every baby or cover all situations.
Management problems arise with babies and children and
the way in which the care-giver responds and co-operates to
resolve them will prove or disprove your first impressions
of her.

Tell the care-giver at the outset that your baby should

not be put to sleep on her tummy or with a pillow, or left feeding from a propped-up bottle. These basic feeding/sleeping directions will usually be followed without question but it is worth stating them anyway.

Management problems might arise such as:
- The baby failing to **gain weight** steadily: Perhaps the baby is a slow or windy feeder, and not finishing bottles. Patience is required. Check she is not being rushed in her feed.
- The baby getting too **fat**: Perhaps she is eating biscuits or crusts to ease teething. Substitute a frozen water-filled teething ring to chew on, provide these for the care-giver.
- Too many **bottles** along with solid food, or too much solid food. Read about nutrition and talk to the care-giver.
- If the baby seems to be too **sedentary**: advise the care-giver that the child needs to roll and move about in a playpen, with stimulatory material such as a mobile, soft ball or rattles. Suggest that the baby needs to be played with more.
- If the baby is **crying** a lot: May be colic, needs comfort. Will grow out of it by around twelve weeks.
- If the baby is **not sleeping** at night: The baby is sleeping too much during the day. Suggest to the child-minder that more stimulation, play, cuddling and fresh air is needed for the child.
- **Skin rashes:** The baby may be sensitive to washing powder. Advise use of non-biological products. Use cotton next to skin, and fine wool outer clothes.
- If the baby is **too hot.** Use cellular blankets and avoid synthetic fabrics. If this persists, consult doctor and have allergy tests.
- **Constipation:** (Hard, strained bowel movements) Tell care-giver to give boiled water or fruit juice.
- **Diarrhoea:** If accompanied by vomiting is serious. Get a preparation from the chemist and give it continuously to avoid dehydration.
- **High temperature:** Strip the child to vest, and sponge down with a cool (not freezing) sponge or flannel. Give cool, boiled water and consult doctor if high temperature persists and a second feed is refused.
- **Foreign objects:** Great care must be taken to avoid poking

cotton wool buds into the baby's ear — these are only to be used on outer folds. Swallowing small objects, or poking them up nose or in ear — consult a doctor.

- **Nappy rash:** More frequent nappy changing required. Leave baby (on a towel) without a nappy in a warm temperature, for periods.
- Any management problem which persists should be discussed with a doctor. The public health clinic, because they see babies and pre-school children in great numbers, are also a good resource.
- **Failure to smile** and respond, or to gain weight, frequent recurring ear, nose, throat or eye infections; continuous squinting up to six months (most babies squint intermittently in the early months) or squinting after six months; persistent rashes; frequent vomiting or chronic constipation are medical problems and need a doctor's attention.

Observe the **baby's development** and do not be lax about having the child attend the public health clinic for the routine developmental checks. When playing with the baby, watch out for her ability to follow movement, grasp toys, follow and look for a toy dropped on the floor, pass a block from one hand to another, attempt to hold a bottle.

While there is great individual variation in the age at which babies sit up, roll over and crawl, nevertheless, if a baby seems behind in several areas, you must ask whether she is getting enough interaction and stimulation. Talk about your observations to the care-giver and ask for her suggestions. She may put your mind at rest from her experience with children, but she may have noticed a lack of progress also, and have been waiting for you to raise the subject. If in doubt, get advice from the public health clinic or your doctor. If something is not right, the earlier it is picked up and action taken, the better.

You might feel that your baby is **neglected** during the day. If you find a very wet nappy when you collect her, or if you find food particles in the folds of the neck or on the hands, or cold feet or hands, or general listlessness, unresponsiveness or failure to thrive, these might indicate neglect. Call to the care-giver unexpectedly during the day and check if there are too many babies being cared for. Tell the care-giver what you have noticed and ask that they be put right. Remember, failure on your part to bring matters of standards of care or hygiene or lack of stimulation and interaction to the care-giver's attention will be interpreted as a sign that you are quite satisfied with things as they are. If things don't improve and come up to your expectations, consider alternative arrangements.

If toddlers and older children **go off their food** or show signs of reverting to more **babyish behaviour,** such as bedwetting or excessive thumb-sucking, or express fear or unwillingness to go to the care-giver, you must investigate. Has anything frightened them? Have they been threatened or shouted at? Are they being bullied? Talk to the care-giver and try to find the cause and work together towards a solution.

If you notice **inappropriate attention-seeking behaviour** such as biting, kicking or spitting, or excessive clinging, your child might be telling you that she needs more attention and interaction and is feeling lonely or left out. Try and give her your undivided attention in greater amounts in the mornings, evenings and at weekends, and discuss your anxiety with the care-giver, so that she will respond similarly.

Temper tantrums are often dismissed as a normal part of 'the terrible twos' and to some extent that is true. They are the child's way of saying 'I've had enough! I've got a mind of my own, but I haven't got the verbal ability to tell you exactly what's annoying me.' Sometimes, when a placid, biddable toddler turns two, the frustration of seeing more demanding children always getting attention and interaction before her, arouses the innate sense of justice and she will not stand for this any longer. Tantrums are thrown.

Having a tantrum means that the child is out of control. Her emotions are beyond comprehension, maybe even to herself. Orders to stop or threats of sanctions are likely to inflame the situation. Keep calm and lift the toddler from behind. Talk quietly and soothingly and think of a compromise, without acceding to the demand. When calm is restored, offer plenty of reassurance that while you find tantrums wearing and unacceptable, you still love the toddler.

If they only occur in one environment, for example, at home, is there something causing this frustration to build up during the day? If they only happen in the day care setting, they could be a protest about not seeing enough of you at home. But this may not necessarily be the case.

Tantrums are rarely simply connected to the immediate stimulus which provokes them, such as being refused a biscuit or putting on wellies. Tantrums could be a response to jealousy of a new baby, or older children persistently taking toys or interfering with play, or teasing.

Discuss the method of dealing with tantrums with the care-giver. Agree a policy of not giving in, which only reinforces the child's belief that tantrum-throwing is a successful tactic to employ, to get her own way.

If children **feel really left out,** they will go to any lengths to force interaction with parents or care-givers. Even negative interaction is preferable to them than no interaction at all, and the child who seeks attention by whatever means must be given attention and time should be spent individually with them until self-esteem is reasserted.

It is wise to ignore a single episode of **bedwetting** or other regressive behaviour, or at least not to make a big issue of it, or discuss it with others in front of the child. Only if a pattern emerges should parents and care-giver put their heads together to identify possible reasons and to work out a solution.

Behavioural problems usually disappear when this combined approach is taken, or the child may simply grow out of them. Increasing language ability by two-and-a-half or three helps children to talk about what's annoying them and they must be encouraged to do so.

If a particular behaviour persists, or becomes worse or unmanageable, it is time to consult a doctor, or the public health clinic for advice and possible referral to a child guidance unit.

Child abuse check

Following the United Nations Convention on the Rights of the Child, the Irish Society for the Prevention of Cruelty to Children has published a Children's Rights Charter. It is quoted here as a guidance for you, the parents, so that from the earliest age you will communicate to your children that you are open to discussion, and that nothing is too silly or too terrible for your children to talk to you about, if it is worrying them.

Every child has the right -
- to a chance to grow in health, safety and opportunity.
- to receive tender loving care from all adults, especially their parents.
- to a childhood.
- to pass safely through childhood.
- to be listened to and taken seriously by adults.
- to have their material, emotional and educational needs adequately catered for.
- to trust their own instincts and feelings.
- to privacy.
- to say no to unwanted touch or affection.
- to reject physical punishment or emotional abuse.
- to question adult authority and say no to adult demands and requests which are wrong or unreasonable.
- to take any measures necessary if they feel under serious threat.
- to refuse gifts.
- to have a real say in who should look after them and how they are cared for.
- not to keep bad secrets.
- to be treated with the same respect and dignity as any adult.
- to ask for help.
- to an education free from bullying, intimidation and fear.
- to independent legal representation in court proceedings of either a criminal or civil nature.
- to age-appropriate factual sex education from birth through adolescence, not to be inappropriately or prematurely sexualised by adults or the media through pornography or a lack of societal vigilance or

understanding of childhood development.
- not to be criminalised within the legal code until such time as they can give informed consent to criminal behaviour (current age of criminal responsibility is seven years; ISPCC recommends fifteen years).
- to be consulted and listened to in all proceedings regarding their future.

Child abuse can fall into four main areas, but they may overlap. These are neglect, emotional abuse, physical abuse and sexual abuse.

Neglect
Neglect describes a situation where children's basic needs for food, clothes, warmth, shelter, hygiene and medical needs are not met. Parents should know if their child is eating a balanced diet, taking account of what is eaten in a day care situation, and what is eaten at home.

- Children who have got their sleeves, clothing or shoes and socks wet during water play or bathroom accidents should not be left wet, and should be changed after the activity is finished.
- Heat and ventilation are to be considered as an important part of the child's environment, particularly when a child is in full day care, with little opportunity for outdoor play during winter months.
- Children should be watched for infestations of head-lice or worms and need to be bathed and have their hair washed at least weekly.
- Their finger and toe nails need regular clipping.
- Their shoes and socks should be well-fitting. The cause of repeated infections or illnesses should be sought and addressed.
- Children are entitled to a safe environment, well lit, with appropriate toys and furniture and without potential danger from burns or falls, access to roads or where unknown adults can have access to them.
- They need space to move about freely without banging into other children, adults or furniture, or being banged into by others.

- They need hygiene, comfort and reasonable quiet in which to sleep.
- Adults and other children are less likely to seek out and interact with a child who is dirty or smelly, or who always has a runny nose.
- Neglect can leave a child with a poor self-image, which makes her more vulnerable to teasing or bullying by other children and more easily enticed into danger.

Emotional abuse

Emotional abuse starts when a child's need for love is not met. The performance of the physical caring tasks alone — feeding, changing, washing — will not be sufficient. These tasks must be carried out with respect and care, without impatience or the implication that they are a bother. Babies and children need to be talked to, smiled at a lot, engaged in verbal and physical play, sung songs to and above all, cuddled frequently and comforted when tired or upset or ill. They need to be conversed with and encouraged to talk. When they show signs that they have had enough of a particular activity, the adult should discontinue it. They should not be frightened, shouted at, teased or taunted by adults or other children, threatened or continually criticised or ridiculed. They should not be encouraged to show-off, nor have their talents exploited by adults.

To develop confidence and self-esteem, children need approval, encouragement and above all, love. They must be told and shown by affectionate interaction that they are loved. Without love, children become nervous or withdrawn, and may grow into cold, uncaring, emotionless and unhappy outsiders, who have difficulty in forming and sustaining relationships at school, work, socially and emotionally.

Physical abuse

Physical abuse is when a child is physically hurt or injured. People who were slapped or otherwise physically hurt as punishment during their own childhood may consider it normal or beneficial, but the grossly unfair advantage of size and strength should make adults question the practice.

111

Adults should ask what they hope the children will learn by physical punishment. Very few situations in life can be sorted out with a punch.

All physical hurt must be ruled out of any day care setting by the parents at the outset. This includes smacks, slaps, pinching, hair-pulling, squeezing, pulling by the arm, or threats of these things, or physical isolation in the corner or being put into any form of coventry.

An explanation should be given, unsought, by the care-giver for any marks or bruises on a child, and parents must always be satisfied with the explanation. Frequent accidents could indicate overcrowding or a negligent attitude in the day care situation, or bullying by another child or children.

Bullying is a combination of physical and emotional abuse. The bully, as well as the victim, needs attention. The victim may be too frightened to tell, but parents should be aware of possible signs:
- Fear of going to day care or school, or refusal to go at all
- Coming home with clothes or books torn
- Becoming withdrawn, not eating, stammering or night-mares
- Unexplained cuts or bruises
- Ducking when approached
- Possessions or pocket money going missing, and unlikely explanations offered

• Older children may steal money from home to pay off the bully

Because of the apparent increase in bullying and in the severity of the tactics used by bullies, the subject has been addressed in books, where parents and child caregivers can learn to understand the needs of the victim and the bully, and take remedial action. (See Appendix IV, Useful books).

Sexual abuse

The increased awareness of child sexual abuse and the relative openness with which it can be discussed, has produced guidelines for prevention and response which parents and care-givers should be aware of.

Prevention techniques should be understood by parents and relayed to children in such a way as not to make them overly afraid.

From the earliest age, children must be made aware of their right to bodily integrity, which is why it is so important that great respect is shown when simply changing a baby's nappy or blowing their nose.

Children should not be pressurised into kissing or even greeting anybody if they show reluctance to do so. These things lay the foundations for knowing that they can say NO to unwanted attentions. They promote the knowledge that children can talk to trusted adults about anything which is troubling them, confident that they will be believed and helped.

Children should be told that it is quite right to scream, shout, kick, punch, lie or run away if they don't like what is happening, or if they feel that they are in danger.

They should have a clear explanation of the difference between a bad secret and a good secret. A bad secret is accompanied by threats that something bad will happen if the secret is told, and often that the other person has some magical power to hurt the child if she tells. A good secret is about something nice – like a present bought for granny, and kept secret until the birthday arrives. Bad secrets should be told to a trusted adult without fear.

Children should be taught to say NO if an adult or older child does the following:

• Offers them a treat or sweets

113

• Offers to buy them something that they would really like
• Tries to isolate them from playmates
• Tries to touch them or kiss them in a way they do not like

If lost, they should know to approach another woman with a child or children. Children should be encouraged to express their feelings and taught to trust their instincts which lead them to dislike certain people or approaches. They should be allowed to talk about their bodies and bodily functions without shame.

Parents must always be vigilant about checking references of care-givers and babysitters, and should always trust their instincts or uneasy feelings, and make other arrangements. The importance of doing this, where day care is provided in a private home setting, cannot be over-emphasised. There is a disturbing amount of evidence of abuse by babysitters. Some adolescents are sexually curious, and this may lead to abuse.

If suspicious that a girl or boy is a victim of sexual abuse, contact the local public health nurse, who has right of access to any pre-school child and who can arrange referral to the appropriate special unit. In the case of older children, contact the Director of Community Care for your area.

Suspicion that sexual abuse has taken place could be prompted by the following behaviours, but it must be emphasised that these are not conclusive and may have other causes:

• Regression to more babyish behaviour, such as bed-wetting
• Boldness
• Over-compliance – easily bossed around, the subject of bullying or teasing
• Over-maturity for age, displaying a pseudo-maturity in taking on an adult role and being over-helpful
• Protest against a particular adult, babysitter or care-giver
• Distrust of adults
• Becoming very withdrawn or very aggressive
• Lack of interest in play or interaction with other children
• Complaints of pains or tummy aches which are undiagnosed – no reason found for them.

The following behaviours have been found to relate specifically to sexual abuse:
• Disclosure by a child
• Hints about sexual activity
• Persistent inappropriate sex play, with toys or other children, or sexually aggressive behaviour with others
• Inappropriate knowledge about sex, using adult language, which refers to sexual activity
• Seductive behaviour, such as opening zips
• Extraordinary fear of men
• Excessive attachment to adults
• Excessive fear of settling down at bedtime and/or being left alone with a particular adult
• Unusual reluctance to join in normal activities involving the removal of clothing, such as bathtime or swimming.

Physical indicators may only appear immediately following abuse and it may be some time before a child will disclose or the abuse is suspected. The absence of any physical signs should not lead the adult into disbelieving any child reporting sexual abuse. Any of the following should be investigated:
• Torn, stained or bloodied underclothing
• Foreign bodies inserted in genital or rectal openings
• Bruising or bleeding in genital areas
• Infections or discharges in these areas
• Any marks or bruising on a baby under one year

If a child reports being the recipient of any sexual activity whatsoever, it is vital that they be believed. Children do not lie about sexual approaches and are not capable of describing things beyond their experience.

The adult must try not to display anger or horror or convey their distress to the child, who desperately needs calm reassurance that it was right to tell. Secrecy and instilling fear of the consequences of telling are the weapons of sexual abusers. A burst of outrage in a trusted adult will confirm rather than relieve the child's fear.

If a child says: 'If I tell you something, will you promise not to tell anybody else?' the adult should answer: 'I will keep the secret until tomorrow morning and we will decide together who will be told next.' Children who have been sexually abused have been manipulated and may have learned to become manipulative themselves, so the adult should not get into collusion with the child in promising to keep bad secrets.

The adult should not press for details, but should listen very quietly. If a child starts to tell and cannot continue, the option of drawing or writing could be suggested, if the child is old enough.

It should be anticipated that the child may deny everything the following day. This frequently happens, because a child may feel that having told a trusted adult, that is the end of the matter, and they can begin to block the memory of the abuse.

It is desperately distressing for an adult to have sexual abuse disclosed by a child. Any adult who finds herself in this situation should seek counselling or professional help to cope with the feelings of guilt, frustration or anger which may follow disclosure, both for the adult's own sake and in order to be of ongoing help to the child who trusted them in the first place.

5

Quick reference questions and answers

Question:
Do children suffer by being away from their parents?

Answer:
Psychologists all over the world are carrying out studies to find the answer to this question. Our focus must be to understand children's needs for love and security, stimulation, interaction and respect. We must insist on the highest standards in both the care-givers and the environment in any day care situation, to ensure that these needs are met. Wise parents will give their children absolute priority outside working hours.

Question
Is one type of care better than another?

Answer:
Every day care setting is different, and the personal qualities of the care-giver are what count. Her training and

experience and her commitment to doing the job properly will dictate the environment. What matters most is that the child is happy and developing well. Some children have no problem with being cared for with a large group, and others may thrive in a small family day care setting.

Question:
Will my baby get enough attention?

Answer
Ideally, a baby during the first year of life should have continuous care from a loving care-giver, with whom a relationship develops. A care-giver should not be responsible for more than three babies. A baby should show signs of continuous progress in all areas of development. Sufficient cuddling, conversation and stimulation cannot be available to a baby where too many babies are together, or where the care-giver does not understand and meet these needs. So, again, the answer lies with the personal qualities of the care-giver.

Question:
Will going back to work prevent a proper family relationship from developing?

Answer:
Relationships are built upon loving concern, good communication and listening-skills, and shared activity. Loving concern will make parents aware of the need for quality in the day care environment and ensure that they keep a vigilant eye on both the care-giver and the child's progress. Good communication with the care-giver should lead to a care-sharing partnership.

Listening attentively to the child and showing respect for her feeling and sensitivities are the foundations of good family relationships. Shared activity, doing things which the children enjoy, and later, reading their school books and taking an interest in their sports, hobbies and music all help towards building relationships. Actually doing things together like cycling, camping, fishing, stamp-collecting or cooking really promotes knowledge of each other's personality, strengths and weaknesses as human beings and makes communication easy.

Shared activity encourages children to talk so their parents listen, and to listen when their parents talk. Working parents may wonder where they will find the time to do these things. Making up a packet of instant trifle together, or cycling to the shops for the paper and an ice-pop together are shared activities. An hour here and there, but regularly and uninterrupted, can be a better investment than family holidays. Children need their own time also, just to mess about with their friends or their gear, and shared activity should follow the lead given by the children.

Question:
Will I still be the primary influence on my child?

Answer:
Yes, if you want to be and if you work at sharing your feelings with your child. The child will be influenced by all the role-models in her life and by what they do rather than by what they say. The child will seek information and guidance from parents, if the parents make a habit of good listening. Resist asking a dozen questions, or rushing in to finish a sentence when your child is struggling to explain something. Look into your child's eyes and do not be distracted by dirty hands, untidy hair or undone shoe laces. Show the child that the doors of communication are open wide and her concerns are your concerns. We are all influenced by people we respect, and ultimately we respect people who respect us.

Question:
Is it really safe to pass responsibility for my child to strangers?

Answer:
Parents sharing the care of their children are not passing responsibility for their children's well-being and development to anybody. Parents must check out the references given by potential care-givers, nannies, child-

minders and satisfy themselves as far as is possible as to the character and suitability of the care-giver. They must be constantly vigilant and at times trust their instincts if they have a feeling that things are not right.

The good care-giver appreciates the need for close co-operation and communication with the parents and does not misinterpret parents' vigilance as criticism of her. If parents have doubts about the quality of the care their child is getting, they must take responsibility for addressing the issue, finding a satisfactory resolution and making the ultimate decision to make alternative arrangements if doubts persist. It is the parents' responsibility to turn the relationship with the care-giver from 'stranger' to care-sharing partner. Being dictatorial or unapproachable, or seeing the care-giver as somehow inferior to the parents prevents the appropriate relationship from developing. The logical outcome is a confused child, with a succession of care-givers. Parents, therefore do not hand over responsibility or remain strangers with the care-giver.

Question:
Children in day care always seem to be sick.

Answer:
General statements like this are impossible to confirm or deny! Young children grouped together, just as school children or adults working together, are very likely to pick up coughs and colds from each other. The children's environment should be warm, well-ventilated and not over-crowded. Care-givers should understand and practice good hygiene. Our climate forces small children to stay indoors most of the time during the winter and household dust can produce coughs and runny noses. Day nurseries in Sweden are now reverting to the old-fashioned practice of putting babies, well wrapped up, to sleep outdoors in their prams. We must wait and see if this practice will reduce the level of minor infections.

Generally, children will not be accepted into a day care setting without having been vaccinated against the serious childhood illnesses. Parents are asked not to bring a child with a raised temperature to a day nursery. Repeated bouts of infections or gastro-enteritis should make parents question the hygiene practice at home or in any day care setting.

Question:

I hear so much conflicting advice, I never know if I'm doing the right thing for my child. I wish there were classes for parents!

Answer:

There are! And many well written, down-to-earth books about babies and children are available. All childcare classes (choice of evening classes available) welcome parents as participants, dads as well as mums. Years ago people learned childcare from observation within the extended family and from the neighbours and friends. Working parents don't have time to spend hours chatting to other parents, exchanging information and tactics, so books and classes are an alternative resource.

As children come towards the end of the primary school cycle, many schools organise a series of talks on adolescence and how to negotiate the family through the process. The rule of thumb for parents when they feel inadequate in the face of a problem is to put themselves in the child's shoes and try to understand the reason for the difficult behaviour or the tears. They should then treat the child and the problem as they themselves would wish to be treated.

Remember that each parent and each child is an individual with varying levels of patience, self-confidence, intelligence and so on. What works in one family would not necessarily work in another. Trust your instincts as a parent, no matter who gives you advice to the contrary and let your children know that you love them and accept them in their human imperfections. Be realistic, and expect that your children will eventually turn out more or less like you in matters like intelligence, achievement, integrity and outlook, when they emerge from adolescence with their own identities as young adults.

Question:

I need to work. Why do I feel so guilty about leaving my child?

Answer:

The reasons for the feelings of guilt are both instinctive and cultural. Most parents instinctively want to nurture and protect their children. In the past, women have been deprived of equivalent education to men which had the effect of making motherhood and home-making the career option and means of self-fulfilment for women. Many factors have changed this. Attitudes are slower to change and working women are still viewed somewhat critically by their parents' generation, and sometimes by full-time, home-making contemporaries. Guilt, as an emotion, cannot be helped, but when it surfaces it must be dealt with at a rational level or it may lead to unwise and unproductive responses, such as turning a blind eye to any shortcomings in the day care arrangement, or spoiling the children with excessive amounts of toys and treats. It must not be allowed to gnaw away self-esteem as a parent, reducing the ability to say 'No' to a child, or to challenge a teacher or care-giver if the child's needs are not being met.

While it is impossible to prevent feelings from happening within ourselves, we certainly can take a firm stand if somebody tries to impose their feelings on us using veiled or even open criticism. If parents need to work, they should expect support and encouragement from family and friends, not criticism. Parents who are bothered by guilt — and most parents are from time to time — should turn it into a useful prompt to set aside time now, this evening, to involve themselves with their children in some appropriate shared activity.

Question:
Will I always feel so guilty?

Answer:

Hopefully not! As the child grows and develops and verbal communication becomes easier, parents are reassured. If they were not working, their children would spend the greater part of the day at school anyway. The worst words in a parent's vocabulary from a child's viewpoint are 'Not now!' 'Now' is the only time that is relevant to a child and postponement can mean death to communication. Using

'Not now' frequently leads to 'If only' and the door is opened for guilty feelings to sneak in. Parents and children are human beings and perfection is not possible in either. Parents will be wise to decide and give priority to what is important for their children and not allow themselves to agonise and torment themselves into a sea of self-doubt.

Question:

My child seems to be getting on fine with the childminder, but I have heard complaints from other parents.

Answer:

Any queries raised about childcare must be examined by the parents. The nature of the complaint should be assessed as being either major or minor. Major complaints can be sub-divided into:
  • Activities on the childminder's part (or any care-giver's) which would expose the children to danger, such as leaving them unattended, carelessly leaving doors or gates open, or leaving bleach or medicines within reach.
  • Activities or approaches which would affect the children's development such as slapping or shouting, or leaving the baby in a cot or high chair all day.

Minor complaints are generally caused by difference in outlook between parents and care-giver, such as emphasis on table manners, tidiness, speaking gramatically or too much TV.

Major complaints must be brought to the attention of the care-giver and a firm commitment given to the parents that they will not recur. Minor complaints can be dealt with between parents and children directly, without undermining the standing of the care-giver in the children's eyes. The parents could use humour to get a message across to the care-giver in a non-threatening way. In the long term, children are more likely to imitate their parents' speech and social habits. The motivation for complaints from other parents must be looked at. Are they looking for moral support in a situation where the issue is clearly best kept as a private discussion between those parents and the childminder, or is it a serious complaint which must be verified and addressed by all parents of the children involved? Parents are often caught between the desire to avoid chopping and changing the day care for less than very valid reasons, and living with doubt about the suitability of the arrangement.

Question:

My sister/friend/neighbour has taken up childminding and she needs the money. Should I change my children to her?

Answer:

She may need the money, but may not necessarily have the attributes of a good childminder. These are the kinds of decisions which only parents themselves can make. But external social pressures should not be the motivation for changing childcare arrangements where the children are happy and with which the parents are satisfied.

Question:

My mother stayed at home with us as children, and keeps making remarks suggesting that a mother's place is in the home.

Answer:

You probably won't be able to change your mother's attitude, so the best policy is to change the subject. Refuse to be drawn into a discussion which leads nowhere and will only wear you both out. Worse still, it may aggravate guilt which you are just learning to deal with positively.

Question:

I've heard that day nurseries have a very organised and structured daily routine. Will my child have enough freedom?

Answer:

Obviously, when catering for a group of children the day must be structured and organised so that the children have variety. This enables the shy children to participate and out-going children to learn patience and co-operation. But day nurseries are not like school, where children have no choice about what happens next and where talking is restricted.

In day nurseries children can move about freely and select the toys or activities they like, and also the children they prefer to play with. Some nurseries are more rigid in adhering to structures and timetables than others. Staff ratio, the actual size of the building and the number of square metres per child will reflect the degree of individual freedom allowed to the children. Nursery staff generally are aware that children need much more than a place of safe containment. But parents should look out for access to a garden with the possibility of play with large toys, swings and climbing frames.

Question:

At what age is my baby old enough to go to day nursery?

Answer:

Take as much maternity leave as possible. Some nurseries have a lower age limit, such as three months or six months. If you are breast-feeding, remember that a baby cannot be weaned suddenly and three to four weeks is required. You may wish to continue with the morning and bedtime feeds after returning to work. This is fine for some mothers but not all. For the parents' sake, as well as for the baby's, the baby should have reached the stage of sleeping through the night after the 10 pm feed, until around 7 am before you return to work, and this varies from one baby to another.

Question:

When my child started with the childminder\in the day nursery, the numbers were fine, but now more children have been taken on and I think it has become too crowded.

Answer:

Childminders should be able to take the children out with them for at least a period during the day, perhaps when older children are at school or play-school. Check the adult/child ratio in the day nursery, which must meet the insurance requirements. Bearing in mind the size of the premises and the space occupied by extra adults as well as extra children, decide if the children have enough room to move about freely and play. If you are not satisfied, raise the matter with the childminder or the nursery manager, with the support of other like-minded parents. Never be afraid to raise any matter in the day care arrangement with the care-giver, because none are without problems from time to time. Problems are best discussed and addressed by parents and care-givers and ironed out, rather than moving the child every time a difficulty is encountered. Remember, as in any business arrangement, silence is taken to mean consent or tacit agreement that all is well.

Question:

I'm exhausted and have no energy to play with my children at the end of the day. I can't wait to put them to bed.

Answer:

The demands of working full time and running a home are colossal, even with today's labour-saving devices in the kitchen. If things are getting on top of you, tell yourself you are wonderful to do all that you manage to do, and go to bed early with a pencil and paper and answer these questions honestly.

- Am I losing weight, or am I ill – have I seen a doctor lately?
- Should I get a good tonic or vitamin supplements and take them conscientiously for two weeks and see if I have more energy then?
- Have I given up taking exercise because I never seem to have the time? (Resolve to walk briskly for twenty minutes at lunchtime or before going to bed at least five times each week. If possible, get back to some sport that you've dropped.)
- What do I find most wearing? shopping? laundry? cooking? housework? (List them out in order of most hated.)
- Can I get somebody into the house, even for a few hours each week to clean or iron?
- Can I pay a friend to cook and pack meals for the freezer

or can I simplify things by doubling up on the cooking at weekends?
- Do I expect too much from myself and brush aside offers of help from partner or family? (List what offers you've had, or who you could call on.)
- Am I getting stressed by doing more than my fair share at work? (List what your job entails and then list what is above and beyond the call of duty and resolve to discuss the matter at work.)
- Do I allow myself to be imposed on socially? (Say no to any requests for voluntary work for a while and opt out of entertaining family and friends.)
- Do I plan my leisure time to ensure I'm doing what I enjoy and with people who are stimulating rather than draining? (Write down how you will spend next Saturday, and then revise it to suit *you*.)

At the end of the day, children are tired and are very demanding of their parents' attention. They pick this time to act up, having behaved themselves all day, and test you to prove to themselves that you really love them, no matter how disruptive they are! This is not the time to start clearing the breakfast things and cooking the dinner. It is the time for a half-hour tune-in to the children. Don't make a big deal about it. Let them decide whether it is to be horse-play or a chat or a story or a cuddle at the TV. But take the phone off the hook and let everything else wait until the day's frustrations or celebrations are worked through. You will find that the time between the meal and bed will be easier and more enjoyable for everybody. As children get older, their co-operation with the household tidying-up will be easily enlisted, when they know that they come first at the end of the day.

Question:
My childminder/nanny is wonderful with the children, but unexpectedly cancels with migraine quite often.

Answer:
Parents usually have a stand-by arrangement for when they or the care-giver is sick, but frequent cancellation at short

notice is difficult. The matter must be talked over together with the care-giver sharing responsibility for an alternative option for the parents. Another local childminder should be found, who is checked out by the parents for suitability, and who is willing to get to know the children and take them for odd sessions, when necessary and with little notice.

Question:
My child won't eat properly in the day nursery.

Answer:
Children's appetites and tastes in food differ and like adults, they do not necessarily eat exactly the same amount of food each day. If children look healthy and are rarely sick and if they are growing steadily and not underweight for their height, then they are eating satisfactorily. They hate being nagged about eating and many children regard meals as a time-wasting chore! Be imaginative! Children who won't eat meat may eat paté or scrambled eggs. If they won't eat cabbage, they may like coleslaw or raw grated carrots. Fresh fruit is as good as vegetables. Present them with tiny portions (they can always have more) because a big full plate may horrify them.

If a child suddenly stops eating or hides food and pretends to have eaten, the reason should be sought and addressed. It could be a plea for attention, bullying, or due to a change of teacher or care-giver. Try and avoid demonstrations of your anxiety or discussing the problem with others in front of the child. Get professional help from a child guidance unit, through your doctor, if you cannot find the reason and remedy it yourself.

Question:
My toddler comes into my bed every night and nobody gets a decent night's sleep.

Answer:
Most children go through a phase of this which passes and the more reassurance you give them, the sooner it will pass. Welcome them into your bed for a cuddle and try and go to

sleep. If that is impossible for you (and partner) then get the toddler to settle with a pillow in a sleeping-bag or wrapped in a duvet on the floor right beside your bed, where you can hold hands or keep your hand on the toddler's shoulder. Leave the sleeping-bag on the floor for a few nights, and the doors open with a light on so that the child understands that you want her beside you if she wakes up. Don't let the child succeed in driving one or other parent from the bed. Never be cross or threatening or offer rewards for staying in their own beds. Children need reassurance when they look for it in this way, and rejection will turn a passing phase into an ongoing nuisance

Epilogue

Being a parent is never easy. The arrival of a baby changes your life in a far more dramatic way than emigrating, moving house or changing job. The fact that the baby is a growing, living person means that her needs will change continually also. As soon as a planned routine is working smoothly, the baby develops new skills or has different needs which disrupt it. For example, leaving a carrycot with a sleeping bundle to granny or a friend for a few hours in the evening is fine until the baby comes to life at midnight, as you drive home. When the baby has outgrown the late night and early morning feeds, and you have readjusted happily to taking a good night's sleep for granted, teething starts!

We have spoken about children's needs so frequently throughout this book that the word 'needs' may have become somewhat diminished through over-use. Wise parents will tune in to their children's needs, anticipate and respond to them in such a way as to forestall difficulties, and when any problem arises, they will deal with it, getting advice if necessary, before it gets out of hand. In every area of life, the extent of any problem is the extent of our ability to cope with it.

Babies and children are human beings, and like the rest of us, vary in temperament and personality. Some thrive on the stimulation of a large group provided in a day nursery, some thrive in smaller groups, or some may benefit most from individual care. This may change as the child matures.

If a child is not settled in and happy with any day care arrangement after a month, parents should examine both the day care and the child's individual personality and consider an alternative.

This book and the suggested reading list will give parents the necessary information to make a choice about day care. You will have ideas of your own to add to the suggested qualities you would like to find in a care-giver or a day nursery. Armed with this book as a guide, you are now sufficiently well-informed to make a decision about which day care will suit you and your child. Knowledge is power and it is hoped that as a parent you now feel empowered to find and recognise quality care. You should have the courage and self-confidence to keep a critical eye on the quality of your child's environment and to raise any matter, which you think needs attention, with the care-giver.

Children are a blessing and a source of great fun and joy. The anxious moments and the worries they bring are far outweighed by the continuous adventure of watching them grow and the pleasure in guiding them to maturity, to reaching their individual goals and achieving their potential.

When you meet their real needs for love and approval, and insist on those as priorities in any day care setting, your children will grow up with self-respect, integrity, confidence and courage, and will become your friends for life.

Appendix I

Contract between parents and childminder/day nursery

The following matters should normally be agreed between parents and childminder or day nursery, and both should keep a copy of the agreement.

- Name, address and phone number of childminder or day nursery

- Details of insurance policy

- Deposit payable in advance - (It may be a booking fee and not refundable)

- Hours covered by the agreement

- Late collection arrangements: fee

- Fees: whether daily, weekly or monthly, manner of payment and date on which payment is to be made

- Charges made when child is absent through illness or for other reason

- Days on which service not available - bank holidays, childminder's or day nursery holidays

-Details of what is included in the service: meals, preparation of bottles, laundry, trips and treats

-Notice or payment in lieu of termination of the arrangement

-Permission to give specific medication

-Refusal to accept children who are ill

-Freedom for parents, grandparents or other relatives to call, by arrangement

-Any special needs the child may have

-Any special arrangements particular to the parents, such as taking the child to the public health clinic, should be included in the agreement, and the agreement should be signed by both parents and childminder.

Appendix II

Information about a child

Information about a minded child for childminder, day nursery/care provider.

- Child's full name, and pet name, if one is used, and date of birth
- Child's address and home phone number
- Family religion
- Parents' work phone numbers, giving all lines and extension numbers
- Parents' place of work
- Name, address and telephone number of close relative to be contacted in an emergency
- Family doctor's name, address and telephone number
- Name of person or persons with authority to collect the child
- Outline of the child's present daily routine
- Any special needs the child may have
- Any fears or phobias
- Dates of various immunisations and vaccinations
- Relevant medical history, allergies, speech, hearing or sight defects
- If the child is on medication, for what reason
- Any previous separations from parents, hospitalisation
- Any other necessary information

Appendix III
Useful addresses

National Childminding Association of Ireland
10 Marlborough Court,
Marlborough St., Dublin 1.
Tel 2875619

National Children's Day Nursery Association
Carmichael House, Nth.
Brunswick St., Dublin 7.
Tel 8722053

Irish Pre-School Playgroups Association
19 Inn's Court, Winetavern St.,
Dublin 8.
Tel 6719245

Naionraí – **Irish Speaking Pre-school Playgroups, An Comhchoiste Reamhscolaiochta Teo.**
7 Merrion Sq.,
Dublin 2.
Tel 6763222

Montessori Teacher Training College (AMI)
Newtownpark Ave.,
Blackrock,
Co. Dublin
Tel 2889717

Montessori Education Centre (Teacher Training)
41 North Great Georges St.
Dublin 1.
Tel 8721581/8726301

London Montessori Training Centre
22/23 Holles St.,
Dublin 2.
Tel 6767761/ 6767730

Barnardo's National Children's Resource Centre
Christchurch Sq.,
Dublin 8.
Tel 530355

Irish Society for the Prevention of Cruelty to Children,
20 Molesworth St.,
Dublin 2.
Tel 6794944

OMEP - Worldwide Organisation for Early Childhood Education C/O ISPCC

Child Sexual Abuse Units:
North City: St Clare's Unit,
Children's Hospital,
Temple St.,
Dublin 1.
Tel 8745214

South City: St Louise's Unit,
Our Lady's Hospital for Sick Children,
Crumlin,
Dublin 12.
Tel 558220

The CARI Foundation (Centre for Abused Children)
110 Lower Drumcondra Rd.,
Dublin 9.
Tel 308529

National Rehabilitation Board,
25 Clyde Rd.,
Ballsbridge,
Dublin 4.
Tel 6684181/6609544

Childcare colleges

College of Catering,
Cathal Brugha St, Dublin 1.
Tel 8747886

Portobello School of Child Care
40 Lower Dominic St.,
Dublin 1.
Tel 8721277

Liberties VEC,
Bull Alley St., Dublin 8.
Tel 540044/540082

Dundrum College,
Sydenham Rd., Dublin 14.
Tel 2982340

FAS Training Centre,
Loughlinstown, Co. Dublin.
Tel 2821811

National College of Childcare and Further Education
The Power House, Pidgeon House Harbour, Dublin 4.
Tel 6687155/ 386050/2896187/ 6680813

The School of Practical Childcare
UCD Blackrock Campus,
Carysfort Ave.,
Blackrock,
Co Dublin.
Tel 2822625/977995

*Employment agencies
specialising in childcare
workers*

Mary Breslin International
8 Carysfort Ave., Blackrock,
Co. Dublin. Tel 2884477

Euro Placement
108 Upper Leeson St., Dublin 2.
Tel 6603926

Au pair agencies

**Annalivia School of
Languages**
19 - 23 Exchequer St., Dublin 2.
Tel 6714433

**Bluefeather School of
Languages,**
35 Montpelier Parade,
Monkstown,
Co Dublin.
Tel. 2806288

Linguaviva Language School,
45 Lower Leeson St.,
Dublin 2.
Tel 789384/612106

Dublin School of English Ltd.
11 Westmoreland Street,
Dublin 2.
Tel 6773221

**The Language Centre of
Ireland,** 9/11 Grafton Street,
Dublin 2.
Tel. 6716266/6716891

Stephanie Maher,
22 Villiers Rd., Rathgar, Dublin
6. Tel 971998

Tax & PRSI/NI Information

Employer Control Section,
Inland Revenue, Lyon House,
28 - 32 Upper O'Connell St.,
Dublin 1.
Tel 8746821

Insurance

**Church & General Insurance
Co Ltd,**
15 Marlborough St., Dublin 1.
Tel 8735111

*Voluntary Bodies & Support
Groups*

**Association for the Welfare of
Children in Hospital**
21 Leinster Lawn, Clonskeagh,
Dublin 14.
Tel 2697108

Asthma Society of Ireland,
24 Anglesea St., Dublin 2.
Tel 6716551

**Blind (National Council for
the Blind of Ireland)**
49 Whitworth Rd.,
Drumcondra,
Dublin 9.
Tel 307033

Central Remedial Clinic
Vernon Ave., Clontarf,
Dublin 3.
Tel 332206

**Cherish - One Parent and
Single Parents' Association,**
2 Lower Pembroke St.,
Dublin 2.
Tel 6682744

**Clanwilliam Institute -
Psychological Assessment**
18 Clanwilliam Tce., Grand
Canal Quay, Dublin 2.
Tel 6761363/6762881

Coeliac Society of Ireland
Carmichael House, Nth.
Brunswick St., Dublin 7.
Tel 8721471

**Comhchoiste Naisíunta na
gColáistí Samhraidh,
Gaeltacht Summer Schools**
46 Kildare St., Dublin 2.
Tel 6794780.

**Cot Death (Irish Sudden
Infant Death Association)**
Carmichael House,
Nth. Brunswick St.,
Dublin 7.
Tel 8735702,
or 34 Sycamore Rd.,
Meadowbrook,
Dundrum,
Dublin 16.
Tel 8747007.

**Cystic Fibrosis Association of
Ireland**
24 Lower Rathmines Rd.,
Dublin 6.
Tel 962433/962186

Deaf (Irish Deaf Society)
Carmichael House, Nth.
Brunswick St., Dublin 7.
Tel 8721233

**Down's Syndrome
Association of Ireland**
5 Fitzwilliam Place, Dublin 2.
Tel 6769255/6769263

**Diabetic (Irish Diabetic
Association)**
82/83 Lower Gardiner St.,
Dublin 1.
Tel 363022

**Dyslexia (Irish Association for
Children and Adults with
Learning Disabilities)**
Suffolk Chambers, 1 Suffolk St.,
Dublin 2.
Tel 6990276

**Eczema (National Eczema
Society)**
Carmichael House, Nth.
Brunswick St., Dublin 7.
Tel 557807

**Epilepsy (Irish Epilepsy
Association)**
249 Crumlin Rd., Dublin 12.
Tel 557500

Federation of Services for Unmarried Parents and their Children
36 Upper Rathmines Rd.
(Above Health Centre),
Dublin 6.
Tel 964155

Gifted Children (Irish Association for Gifted Children)
Carmichael House, Nth.
Brunswick St., Dublin 7.
Tel (After 3 pm), 380565

Gingerbread Ireland
29/30 Dame St., Dublin 2.
Tel 6710291

Hyperactive Children's Support Group Ireland, National Children's Resource Centre,
c/o Barnardos, Christchurch Sq., Dublin 8.
Tel 530355

Mental Handicap (National Association for the Mentally Handicapped of Ireland)
5 Fitzwilliam Place,
Dublin 2.
Tel 6766035

Parents Under Stress Carmichael House, Nth.
Brunswick St.,
Dublin 7.
Tel 8721055

Parents & Friends of Mentally Handicapped Children
St. Michael's House,
Willowfield Pk.,
Goatstown,
Dublin 14.
Tel 2987033

Appendix IV
Useful books

ABC of Day Nurseries in Ireland (1991). Available from Micro Workshop, 22 Crofton Rd., Dun Laoghaire, Co. Dublin. Phone 2806294

Rees, Pat, *Positive Parenting - A Survival Guide* (1992). Attic Press, Dublin.

Jennings, Geraldine, *Successful Day Nursery Management,* (1990). Attic Press, Dublin.

ISPCC Publications: *Childline Handbook for Children in Trouble or Danger.* Kidscape Productions: *'Stop Bullying!', 'Keep Them Safe!'*

Goff, Toni. *Bully for You!* (1991). M. Twinn Swindon.

Compiled by Murray, Barbara, Gallagher, Ann-Marie and Carroll, Hilda, *Directory of Day Care and Day Activity Centres for People with Disabilities* (1990). Available from National Rehabilitation Board, 25 Clyde Rd., Dublin 4.

Byrne, Brendan, *Coping with Bullying in Schools* (1993). Pigeon Publications, Dublin.

Pithers, David and Greene, Sarah, *'We Can Say No' - A Child's Guide* (1990). A Red Fox Book by Arrow Books, Ltd. London.

Hugh Jolly, *Book of Childcare,* (1980). Allen and Unwin, Sydney.

Brant, Prof Herbert and Gilbert, Prof Kenneth, *The Complete Mothercare Manual,* (1991). Conran, Octopus, London.

Shirley, Conran, *The Guide for Everyone who hates Housework,* (1991). Penguin Books, London.

Bibliography

Clarke, Madeleine and Nóirín Hayes, (1991) *Child Care in Ireland - A Parents' Guide.* Gill & Macmillan, Dublin.

Fewell, Rebecca R. Ph.D., (1992) "Childcare for Children with Special Needs" Paper from Johnson & Johnson Pediatrric Institute Symposium 'Day Care for Children' Published in Pediatrics, Jan. 1993, Col 91, No. 1. Part 2.

Gesell, A.L. and Catherine Amatruda, (1974) *Developmental Diagnosis* (3rd edit.) Hilda Knobloch & Benjamin Paramanick (eds.), Harper & Row, New York.

Hoffman, Lois W., and F. Ivan Nye, et al., (1974) *Working Mothers,* Jossey-Bass Publishers, San Fransisco.

Jennings, Geraldine, (1990) *Successful Day Nursery Management,* Attic Press, Dublin.

Schaffer, H.R., (1977) *Mothering.* Fontana.

Stone, Judith, & Felicity Taylor, (1977) *A Handbook for Parents with a Handicapped Child.* Arrow Books, London.

Young, Denis R., & Richard R. Nelson, (1973) *Public Policy for Day Care of Young Children,* Lexington, USA.

Index